D1165755

Giuseppe Garibaldi

A Biography of the Father of Modern Italy

Dr. Benedict S. LiPira

Noble House
Baltimore, Maryland

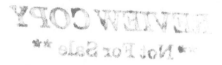
Giuseppe Garibaldi:
A Biography of the Father of Modern Italy

Copyright © 1998 Dr. Benedict LiPira

Library of Congress
Cataloging in Publication Data
ISBN 1-56167-432-X

Library of Congress Card Catalog Number:
98-84760

Published by

Noble House

8019 Belair Road, Suite 10
Baltimore, Maryland 21236

Manufactured in the United States of America

TABLE OF CONTENTS

Prologue	1
Chapter I: Birthplace and Family	4
Chapter II: Young Italy	7
Chapter III: South America/Rio Grande	11
Chapter IV: Anita	16
Chapter V: South America/Costa Bravo	19
Chapter VI: Montevideo	24
Chapter VII: Return to Italy	28
Chapter VIII: Roman Campaign of 1849	34
Chapter IX: Escape/Death of Anita	40
Chapter X: Exile	44
Chapter XI: Risorgimento/Caprera	48
Chapter XII: Cacciatori delle Alpi	53
Chapter XIII: Amorous Adventures	60
Chapter XIV: The Thousand	64
Chapter XV: Invasion of Sicily	69
Chapter XVI: Palermo	74
Chapter XVII: Final Conquest of Sicily	79
Chapter XVIII: Advance to Naples	84
Chapter XIX: Battle of Volturno	90
Chapter XX: Return to Caprera	95
Chapter XXI: Defeat at Aspromonte	99
Chapter XXII: England/Venice	103
Chapter XXIII: Defeat at Mentena	108
Chapter XXIV: French Expedition	112
Chapter XXV: Final Years	118
Epilogue	122
Bibliography	124

LIST OF MAPS

Kingdom of Piedmont, April 1859   3
Regional View of *Garibaldini* Operations in South America   10
Defense of Rome 1849   33
Garibaldi's Retreat from Rome, 1849   39
Caprera - Garibaldi's Home for Twenty-Six Years   52
Garibaldi's Alpine Campaign 1859   59
Sicily 1860   68
Garibaldi's Route to Naples 1860   83
Battle of Volturno 1860   89
Kingdom of Piedmont/Italy, November 1860   94
Kingdom of Italy, November 1870   117

PROLOGUE

Nice, France
Old Town, Wharf
August, 1991

There I was, an American tourist, awestruck in front of Giuseppe Garibaldi's birthplace—a modest three story brick townhouse centrally located at the port of old Nice. Beneath the window sill of the second floor was a plaque written in Italian:

> *Qui di Fronte Era La Casa*
> *Dov' ebbe i Natali il, 4 Luglio 1807*
> *GIUSEPPE GARIBALDI*
> *La Societa' Italiana di Beneficenza*
> *Lasciando Questa Sua Sede*
> *Dopo 46 Anni di Nobile Attiva nel Cinquantenario*
> *Della Morte dell' Eroe a Perrenne Memoria Pose*
> *2 Giugno 1932*

Here before you was the house
In which the birth on July 4, 1807 was
GIUSEPPE GARIBALDI
The Italian Society of Charity left this, its center,
On the 50th anniversary of the death of the hero
After 46 years of noble activity to perpetuate his memory.

2 June 1932

.....and on the first floor was a shop selling windows and siding. What a demeaning commemoration to the birthplace of such a heroic figure of Italian history! But, then, no Hollywood movie or TV mini-series would do justice to glorify such a "superhero." Only the memory in each Italian heart could echo what Garibaldi meant to the republic of Italy.

This is a historical biography of Giuseppe Garibaldi (b. 1807 - d. 1882). The author is not a literary professional, but rather a student of Garibaldi, his life and his adventures. The following manuscript is not presented as a researched historical treatise, but rather a compilation of readings and studies of this historic figure. This was not an easy task, as many historians disagreed as to exact dates and what actually happened on some of the historic events. It is a most prolific story; Garibaldi's accomplishments have affected the history of modern Italy. This writing is mainly for American consumption and to educate the uninformed on this subject.

In 476 A.D., the last Roman Emperor of the West, Romulus Augustulus, was forced to abdicate. Consequently, Constantinople became the seat of a declining Roman Empire. From that time Italy had no political unity and did not exist as a state. Not until 1870, was it again brought under one sovereign. Italy did not blossom as a nation, as we know it, until some ninety-four years after the independence of the United States and did not complete its flowering until the Lateran Agreement with the Vatican in 1929 and designation as a republic in 1946. It is pure speculation as to when Italy would have gained its united status without the outstanding successes of Garibaldi.

Giuseppe Garibaldi was a romantic giant in a fruitful historical period. His story needs to be told to the students of history, for it contains all the elements of American ideals—life, liberty, and the pursuit of happiness.

Piedmont

Lombardy

Venetia

Genoa

Tuscany

Papal
States

Rome

Naples

Kingdom
of
Two Sicilies

Sardinia

Calabria

Palermo

Sicily

Kingdom of Piedmont April, 1859

CHAPTER I: BIRTH PLACE AND FAMILY

Giuseppe Garibaldi was born July 4, 1807 in the aforementioned three story structure by the port of Nice. Nice was ceded in 1815 to the monarchy of Piedmont by the Congress of Vienna by the hand of Austrian Prince Metternich. But in 1807, Nice was under Napoleonic rule. Giuseppe was the second son of Rosa and Dominic Garibaldi. His mother was a simple woman who occasionally worked as a washer woman to aid in the subsistence of the family. (She had seven children.) His father was a successful sea captain whose livelihood was dictated by sailing to the islands of Corsica and Sardinia and to the shores of Africa and western Italy. The senior Garibaldi frequently took the young Giuseppe on some of these trips and instilled the love of the sea into the lad, which stayed a lifetime. He was, by his own definition, first and foremost, a sailor. Little is known about Giuseppe's four brothers and two sisters. However, his older brother, Angelo, inspired in him a fervent desire to learn the inherent language and history of his homeland. Angelo, born in 1804 and also raised as a seaman, evolved into a businessman and later, in Philadelphia, became the Sardinian Consul. Angelo died at the young age of forty-nine in 1853.

Giuseppe was a good student with those subjects that drew his interest; i.e., Roman history, chivalric poems and the verse of Ugo Foscolo—an Italian poet whose prose inflamed the populace with the ideals of the French Revolution. He attended local schools which provided the basic curriculums of the era. He neglected studies in the English language, but concentrated on Italian, its language as well its history. The language he grew up with was the local Ligurian dialect. Of course, French was also spoken in the area and all of these became part of the many languages he was to speak fluently. Thus, with the basics he learned on sea excursions and his early formal education, Giuseppe became attuned to the outside world. Early in his life, he was aware of people's struggles, their hopes and desires for a free life unencumbered by governmental interference and the pursuit of happiness for themselves and their families.

One has to comprehend that these ideals were formulated in an environment of abstract poverty as we know it today. There was no indoor plumbing, no electricity, and, of course, no lighting other than the sun by day and candlelight by night. Electronic devices with which we are familiar today (radio, television, computers, etc.) were not to be realized for another 150 years. Communication with the immediate area was done by word of mouth; with the rest of Europe it took weeks and months before news filtered through the local commune. News from the New World was even more slowly received but with much more skepticism. The local community was only concerned with the daily trials and tribulations with which they had to contend. Politics, they believed, was a luxury of kings and statesmen. In their simple world, there were the extremes of the rich and politically connected and the disenfranchised poor. Every now and then, a great leader would come on the scene and aspire to improve the life of his fellow man. Giuseppe Garibaldi was to be that leader.

His father, son of a sea captain as well, was named Dominic Garibaldi and came from Chiavara, a coastal village south of Genoa. Dominic had hoped Giuseppe would become a lawyer, a physician, or even a priest, but yielded to the youth's adventurous spirit and intense desire for the open sea. At the age of fifteen, Giuseppe was hired on as a cabin boy on the brigantine *Costanza* with the highly regarded captain, Angelo Pesante. This first voyage proved very enlightening as it traveled to Odessa on the Black Sea.

Another memorable voyage was to Rome in 1825 with his father. They stayed in the Eternal City for over a month as his pious father was on a pilgrimage for the Holy Year. Giuseppe was enthralled by ancient Rome, its imperial splendor and pre-

Christian life and values. Rome at its height of glory, he was reminded, was a society of liberated people, ennobled men, and a plethora of teachers and guardians of human rights. Now, he thought, in 1825, Papal Rome smothered all aspirations of nationalism and deferred any preservation of Italy's culture. His personal distrust for priestly education was widened by this observation and this intense antipapal feeling remained with him his entire life. There and then, he envisaged Rome as the cradle of a new Italian nation. He wrote in his memoirs, "The Rome I beheld with the eyes of my youthful imagination was the Rome of the future—the Rome that I never despaired of even when I was shipwrecked, dying, banished to the farthest depths of the American forests—the dominant thought and inspiration of my whole life."

There followed many travels to other lands that led to many tragic events which subjected him to strange cultures and peoples but matured the young man. As mentioned before, he traveled to the Black Sea as well as to Cagliari, Genoa, and ports in the Near East. Many times the ships were seized and plundered by pirates. On one trip, he became ill and had to remain behind in Constantinople. Hostilities with Russia were felt in the Turkish capital and his stay extended to several months. He subsisted by teaching and residing with an understanding family from Nice until he won his way home.

He survived all these trials and finally received his first commission as captain on the *Nostra Signora delle Grazie* in 1832. He sailed with her to Port-Mahon and eventually back to Constantinople renewing friendships he made on his initial trip.

Giuseppe was now his own man, full of ideals and hopes that fill the mind of a young man. He was consumed by any thought of freedom, independence, and the ultimate obliteration of class distinctions in Italy. He was prepared to take the burden of the less fortunate on his shoulders and deliver them to a better life. Of all the dominating forces in his life, the idea of freedom and unification for Italy was to be the strongest.

Chapter II: Young Italy

Italy in 1833 was divided into many provinces and municipalities controlled by European powers. Other areas were governed by native dynasties resistant to change and set against the new doctrines of liberalism and nationalism. Austria was the dominant force on the Italian peninsula after the collapse of Napoleonic rule. (Napoleon Bonaparte abdicated in 1814.) The Congress of Vienna of 1815 ceded Lombardy and Venetia, together with satellite dukedoms in Florence, Modena, and Parma to Austria. Victor Emmanuel I of Sardinia ruled the province of Piedmont, which was a hotbed of Italian independence. The Principality of Lucca was under the control of the Bourbons, who inherited the Duchy of Parma upon the death of Maria Louisa, daughter of the Austrian Emperor. The Grand Duchy of Tuscany was ruled by Leopold II, a nephew of the Austrian Emperor, while the Papacy controlled the States of the Church with the assistance of Austrian troops. In the south, the Bourbon dynasty of Naples controlled the Kingdom of the Two Sicilies but were closely allied with the Austrians. Clearly, in 1833, all of Italy was directly or indirectly under the control of Austria with the exception of Piedmont.

Nationalism was growing in all of Italy, but nowhere as strong as in Piedmont. Previous revolutionary attempts were put down severely by Austrian forces in Piedmont as well as in Naples, the Papal States, and the Duchy of Modena. The repression by the Austrians was swift, ferocious, and ominous. Many of the early patriots lost their lives on the gallows; some were imprisoned and others were exiled. Although they failed, these early efforts inspired a new generation of patriots that were to provide leadership in future attempts. More than anything, the weakness and fragility of the kingdoms and duchies set by the Congress of Vienna was evident; the might of the Austrian army could only keep them intact.

One of those exiled patriots was Giuseppe Mazzini (1805-1872), a son of a Genoese doctor. Arrested by police in Genoa for complicity and membership in the revolutionary secret society *Carbonari*, he was exiled to Marseilles in 1831. There, through his literary endeavors, he rallied his countrymen to thoughts of national unity. Always a staunch Republican, he had little love for the monarchy. He founded the society of Young Italy and published a publication by the same name. Late in 1833, in the suburbs of Marseilles, Garibaldi was taken to meet Mazzini and enrolled in this secret society. He took an oath, in the name of God and the martyrs of Italy, to fight against injustice, oppression, tyranny, and to make an Italian nation one and free.

In 1834, under Mazzini's direction, Garibaldi was involved in a feeble attempt at insurrection in Piedmont. He joined the Piedmont navy as a seaman first-class on the frigate *Eurydice*. His job was to proselytize the crew and eventually take over the ship and place it at the disposal of the Republicans. At the port of Genoa, he left the ship to join his coconspirators at Sarzana Square where the civil uprising was to begin. He soon learned that the plot had failed, many arrests had been made and the remaining Republicans had fled. Garibaldi realized his precarious position and took to flight into the mountains disguised as a fruit vendor. He followed unfamiliar paths westward (a distance of 150 miles) for ten days until he finally arrived at the home of an aunt in Nice. After a night's rest, he ventured into France where he was arrested and taken to the prison at Draguignan. He promptly escaped and fled to Marseilles avoiding capture by consistently talking French and singing French popular songs in full view of the local constabulary. Meanwhile, he was sentenced to death for high treason in absentia by the government of Piedmont.

In those early years, Garibaldi became disenchanted with politically motivated aristocrats who assisted him in his quest for an united Italy. Time and time again, those who were close to the movement of Italian nationalism would disappoint him at the moment their efforts were needed. Political manipulations and compromise were rampant to the chagrin of Garibaldi. To him, when it came to the unity of Italy, appeasement was not a virtue. He envisioned a dictatorial nation, in its early years, but restoring, in time, all rights and privileges in a fully democratic society. Dictatorial, at first, because the populace was not privy to such universal freedom for hundreds of years and depended on outside powers to govern them in the most picayune matters. Italy had been divided for centuries into small states, separated by trade barriers, local customs, varieties of dialect, and interstate jealousies; she was not even fully aware of the movement of prospective unity and any idea of mass movement was completely alien to her way of thinking. After a time, he thought, Italy would be capable of self-government in the true sense of democracy.

Garibaldi resumed his vocation as a seaman from Marseilles, returning to his old routes to the Black Sea and Tunis. It was an unsatisfactory clandestine existence fearing that, at any time, he could be apprehended and sent back to Genoa for execution. During this time, Marseilles and the Ligurian coast were besieged by an epidemic of cholera that brought death and devastation to the young and old, to the rich and poor. Millions were dying each year of this dreaded disease and the healthy were leaving. Many regarded South America as the new promised land; the migration at this time was approaching a million each year. The whole Ligurian coastline was becoming depopulated by migrants escaping deprivation and disease to seek their fortune in the New World. Garibaldi was active in relief and assisted the needy in their time of need with no regard to his well being. Finally, after loss of many friends and relatives and tired of his fugitive status, he realized he must find a new home. In the final days of 1835, Garibaldi boarded the French ship *Nautonnier* in Marseilles for passage to Rio de Janeiro. He was not to return to Italy for thirteen years; Garibaldi was twenty-seven years old.

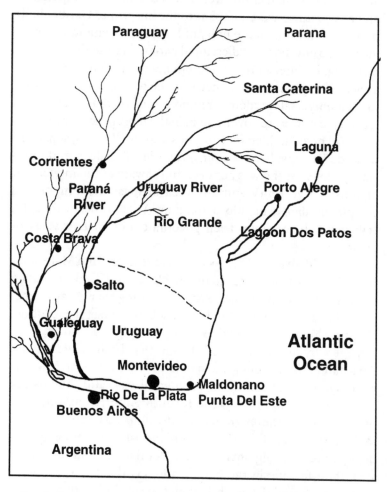

Regional View of *Garibaldini* Operations in South America

CHAPTER III: SOUTH AMERICA/RIO GRANDE

In January 1836, Garibaldi arrived in a country as foreign and remote as any he had visited in his vocation as a merchant seaman. Thankful that there was a pocket of Italian immigrants in Rio Janeiro, he turned to the Italian community for friendship after experiencing intense homesickness. One of these early friends that he regarded as a "brother" was Luigi Rosetti. With Rosetti, Garibaldi ventured into the trading business and traveled up and down the coast selling flour, sugar and brandy. Unfortunately, Garibaldi's business acumen was poor; he was not familiar with the customs and economics of the new land. The venture proved to be unprofitable and short-lived, but most of all Garibaldi was bored.

Brazil had shed itself from Portuguese rule in 1822 but was engaged in civil strife at this time. Its most southern province, Rio Grande, was trying to assert its independence with little accommodation from the new monarchist regime of Brazil. The revolutionary leaders were imprisoned for their efforts. Garibaldi and Rosetti visited these men in prison many times and finally agreed to a noble enterprise in the name of Rio Grande's freedom and liberty.

They outfitted their small trading ship, the *Mazzini*, to be a fighting vessel and aspired to disrupt shipping lines and commerce of Brazilian waterways. Some would say this was sheer piracy, but Garibaldi never raided any ship for any personal material gain. He was adamant about nothing but the most genteel treatment for prisoners, as well as deliverance of booty to the underprivileged. He was too much an idealist and moralist to be tagged as a mere soldier of fortune.

Their first encounter was the brig *Maribondo* and the booty was insignificant. However, in Garibaldi's memoirs, he recalled how he freed some Negro slaves and that one of them, Antonio, a tremendous physical specimen, joined his growing band. Slowly improving on their new avocation, they soon captured the schooner *Luisa* with a sizable cargo of coffee. The pirated ship was larger and more sea worthy than their ship, so they sank the *Mazzini* and headed for the friendly harbor of Maldonano, Uruguay with their new found spoils. At Maldonano, they were greeted as returning heroes and a festive mood was omnipresent throughout the city. Rosetti, in the meantime, traveled to Montevideo to sell the booty and improve their financial position. However, Oribe, the President of the Republic of Montevideo proved to be an antagonist toward the independence of Rio Grande and ordered the immediate arrest of Garibaldi and his associates. Warned of the impending arrest by officials of Maldonado, Garibaldi took to the open sea to rendezvous with Rosetti at Punta de Jesus Maria near Montevideo.

On the morning of June 15, 1837, Garibaldi's ship and crew were put upon by two large ships from the government of Montevideo. They ordered an immediate surrender and maneuvered to board the hostile schooner. Garibaldi, realizing the precarious position, ordered the hoisting of sails in an attempt outrun the war ships. At that moment, a voluminous volley burst forth and many of Garibaldi's crew were instantly killed. One of these, a close friend, Fiorentino, was shot in the face as he tended the rudder. A violent battle ensued as the government forces unsuccessfully tried to board the ship. Garibaldi, sensing the futility of the fight if someone didn't tend to the rudder to facilitate escape, rolled, crawled, and jumped his way to the tiller. Shooting as he moved, he managed to reach the controls when he was struck by a second volley. For a man of lesser constitution, it would have been a fatal blow. The bullet entered his neck from one side and lodged just under his ear on the other side; he slumped unconscious to the deck. The rest of the crew, under the heroic inspiration of Luigi Carniglia, fought valiantly and succeeded in getting the ship into the wind to make good their escape. Garibaldi was in and out of consciousness, losing blood and unable to help his comrades. As Garibaldi lie in a stupor between life and death, his crew dropped the dead into the open sea, wondering whether their captain was to become one of these unfortunates. None had traveled the waters they were forced to sail to elude the government forces. Except for the close bound Italians, fear and confusion gripped the crew and many contemplated surrender. Garibaldi, during a short period of consciousness, feebly rallied his crew and pointed to Santa Fe on the Paraná River as a refuge. Garibaldi wrote, "One can readily imagine my condition during those critical hours. Mortally wounded and unable to move, without help or advice of an aid who knew the land or the waters, I could only cast my dying glances upon our ship's chart, which had been brought to me in order that I might indicate a destination for our journey and course to follow. I pointed to Santa Fe on the Paraná River, simply because the name seemed to me to be printed in larger characters. None of us had ever navigated in that river except Maurizio, who once before had been there. The men, with exception of the Italians, let this be mentioned for the sake of the truth, were overwhelmed with fear and confusion at the sight of my dangerous condition and Fiorentino's body. They were afraid of being captured and treated as corsairs; consequently, they took the first opportunity to desert."

He thought he would never see Italy again. The expressions of the crew as to his condition were solemn. They universally accepted his request not to be buried at sea if he should succumb. His thoughts were of home—family and Italy. Would he ever see his mother again? Would he ever be able to fight for his native land and see it free? If not, he thought, he would be spared the humiliation of seeing Italy fall back into slavery and shame. Despite his daze, he realized he must live to see that this never happened; he must fulfill his destiny.

But there he lie, humbled by a lone bullet, wondering if he, indeed, would live to see another day, another dawn, another sunset. Just thirty years old, he knew he was too young to die. He had a lifetime of loves, desires, and ambitions to realize. Was this all there was to the life of Giuseppe Garibaldi? He was not religious and not in the practice of praying to a higher spirit. However, he did believe in the spiritual being of his fellow man. The strength of character he observed in his compatriots had to be worth something. This ethereal personification had given hope to the oppressed, to the downtrodden. Conviction to the ideals of a free society and strength of mind to promote these ideals, despite any trials and tribulations, was the worth of any man. Garibaldi had to live, live to be an exponent of a free and democratic Italian society, apostolic in the spread of its thesis but Jesuit to bring it to fruition.

After ten days wandering aimlessly up the Paraná River, the schooner limped into Gualeguay, an Argentine village. The Argentines, at this time, were unsympathetic to the conflict raging between Brazil and Rio Grande and received the crew as prisoners of war, but they were not sequestered. Finally, after all this time, Garibaldi had the bullet removed by a surgeon by the name of Ramon dell' Arca. In short time, due to his recuperative powers, he recovered. After six months, the government forces moved to place him in isolation on the Paraná. Aware that this might be a final imprisonment, Garibaldi attempted to escape. However, he was betrayed by his guide, recaptured, shackled, and brought back to Gualeguay. This time the treatment was not too friendly.

He was brought before Governor Millan, who was ruthless in extracting information from captured enemies of the state. This was to be Garibaldi's first experience with intense torture. The governor wanted him to divulge the names of all those who had helped him in his attempted escape. Garibaldi gave nothing. While shackled, he was whipped viciously for hours. Garibaldi gave nothing. Deprived of water and food, he was suspended form a beam in the ceiling with his hands tied above for two hours. Garibaldi gave nothing. Realizing the resistance of his prisoner, Millan allowed Garibaldi to return to his cell, weak and limp.

After a few days, he was transferred to the prison at Bajada. There he was jailed in a dark dank cell for two months. On the intervention of the governor of the province, he was afforded medical treatment and subsequently released early in March 1838. He embarked on a Genovese brigantine to Guazu and eventually boarded a cutter to Montevideo where he rejoined his good friends Rosetti, Carniglia, and Cuneo.

After staying a month, renewing old friendships and living a fugitive existence once again, he was beckoned by the revolutionary forces in Rio Grande. On meeting with President Goncalves, who had escaped from his Brazilian captors, Garibaldi was made commander of the Rio Grande navy, comprised of two cutters. The larger one, *Rio Pardo*, was commanded by Garibaldi, while the other, *Republicano*, was commanded by a United States citizen by the name of John Griggs. Each ship had two cannons and a crew of thirty-five men, hardly a formidable force against the thirty ships of the Brazilian navy. However, the fight was on.

After the small "armada" harassed the Lagoon dos Patos for a few months, the imperialists were astounded by the menacing attacks of this evasive naval force. Encouraged by his successes, President Goncalves ordered Garibaldi to take part in the invasion of Santa Catarina, a province north of Rio Grande. To do this, the tiny force had to mount the ships, *Rio Pardo* and *Republicano*, on oxen driven carts. Each ship was loaded on large wagons drawn by a hundred oxen for a distance of fifty-four miles and put to the open sea. However, off the coast of Santa Catarina, they ran into a violent storm. Griggs' ship was spared, but Garibaldi's *Rio Pardo* sank, tossed aside like a small toy on an angry sea. Being a strong swimmer since his youth, Garibaldi managed to make it to shore despite a strong tide and high waves. He was devastated by the loss of so many of his compatriots. Only fourteen survived from a crew of thirty-five, one of which was his close friend, Luigi Carniglia.

The survivors joined the Rio Grande army in the siege of Santa Catarina which fell on July 23, 1839.

CHAPTER IV: ANITA

It was at Santa Catarina that Garibaldi was ordered back to harass the Imperial fleet along the Brazilian coast. He was fortunate to find a seized gunboat carrying seven guns, a far cry from the one cannon *Mazzini*. As it was damaged due to previous battles, Garibaldi placed it in dry-dock and anxiously awaited the completion of repairs.

One lazy afternoon, as he checked the work in progress, he turned to the beautiful South American landscape with his spyglass. Nothing was particularly eye-catching except for an exquisite panorama of Santa Catarina. All of sudden, a lovely vision appeared in full view. He was dumfounded! There, just offshore, was a young woman hanging her wash in the most routine fashion. Then, as if by command, she straightened up and turned toward the ship and smiled, as if she was attuned to Giuseppe's attention. "What a beauty!" Garibaldi exclaimed. The image in the spyglass made her appear as if she were directly in front of him. He reached out as if to touch her but to no avail. "What a goddess," he proclaimed. Long, lovely black hair cascaded over her delicate shoulders which lead the eye to a diminutive but statuesque torso. But her eyes, such unforgettable pools of loveliness, were large, dark and sparkling which embellished a smile that moved the most reticent. Garibaldi was in love!

He immediately had a boat brought about and was rowed to shore in a matter of minutes, but the girl was nowhere in sight. The homes resembled one another and all had their wash hanging as if deliberately done to confuse him. He searched for hours, but she had disappeared. Despondent and ready to head back to the ship, he ran into a merchant with whom he had previous transactions. The elderly gentleman invited Garibaldi to his house for a cup of coffee and some political debate. He was reluctantly lead to the elderly man's residence and slumped in a chair, disappointed at the lost of his love goddess. Shortly after, a dark skinned young woman entered the room with a tray of coffee. To Garibaldi's surprise, she was the girl he had seen in his spyglass.

Rising to his feet and moving toward her as if in a dream, he said, "Tu devi esser mia!" ("You must become mine!") She was Anita Maria da Silva who as "Anita" was to become a heroic historical figure in her own right. But for now, she slowly approached Garibaldi and nodded with a sparkling smile and an impish wink; she didn't know a word of Italian. This aura of lovesick doves did not impress the elderly merchant. He was her husband!

At this particular moment, the history books take different turns as to what happened next. Garibaldi, in his memoirs, deferred from the actual events concerning this episode in his life. He did, in later years, have deep remorse for taking her away from her homeland at the expense of her husband's hospitality. It seems that after weeks of unsuccessful soliciting to gain the release of Anita, Garibaldi planned an elopement. One moonlit night, a small skiff was rowed to a preordained site near her residence. Garibaldi waited nervously for her arrival, but no one appeared for hours. He waited past midnight as the moon increased its romantic glow over the area. Just as he was to return to the ship and declare the episode a futile cause, he heard someone running through the woods. From a distance he heard (in Spanish), " Giuseppe, I am yours." She fell into his outstretched arms and they declared their life vows to each other as the crew slowly rowed the skiff away on that memorable moonlit night in October 1839. Giuseppe and Anita embarked on an intense love affair that lasted eleven years. She was nineteen; he was thirty-two.

Anita joined Garibaldi in his naval endeavors. Unfortunately, the Brazilians had gathered all their forces to put down the uprising once and for all. The revolutionary forces proved to be no match for the Imperial navy; they were nothing but target practice for the formidable government forces. John Grigg went down with his ship and other losses were building at an alarming rate. Garibaldi burned his ship and retreated with the land forces to the interior, Anita always at his side. They hid in the hills, fighting small skirmishes without exposing themselves to the main Brazilian army for over a year. It was a grim and Spartan existence with constant harassment from the imperialists as well as from the local populace who were losing their fervor for independence. It was under this atmosphere that Garibaldi's first son was born on September 16, 1840. Menotti, named after the famous Italian martyr, was to be an instrumental figure in later years in his father's struggle to free Italy.

Twelve days after Menotti's birth, the farm on which they were living was surrounded by Colonel Moringue's troops of the Brazilian army. Garibaldi was away on a mission leaving Anita home alone with the newborn. With her typical bravado that would brand her for years to come, she snatched up her baby and mounted the closest horse. In a desperate attempt to flee, she jumped out of the corral and streaked for the nearest woodland. She rode for four days and nights to finally elude the pursuing enemy. Garibaldi was in hot pursuit as soon as he was aware of the fate of his family. Knowing the terrain and its people, the family was reunited in a short time.

The situation of the Republican Army was seriously deteriorating from day to day. Large losses and deprivation had accelerated the desertions. The natives of the region had become weary of the many years of armed combat and began withholding support to the revolutionaries. Finally, President Goncalves sent for Garibaldi. The unlucky president had resigned himself to sue for peace. The monarchy of Brazil had offered him the governorship of Rio Grande as soon as all armed resistance was complete and final. Unable to pay Garibaldi any monies for his six years of service, he bequeathed a gift of nine hundred head of cattle The war in Rio Grande was over.

Subsequently, with his family and a few faithful followers, Garibaldi herded his cattle south to Montevideo and to settle down to a peaceful home life. Little did he know what the future had in store.

CHAPTER V: SOUTH AMERICA/COSTA BRAVO

In the spring of 1841, Garibaldi, Anita, and their son, Menotti, arrived in Montevideo with little of the herd. After fifty days of rugged travel across mountainous terrain and through flooded rivers, the herd had dwindled daily. His inexperience as a gaucho did not help. He received little value for the gift that was bestowed upon him in Rio Grande, only one-third of the original number of cattle remained. Garibaldi was not adept as a business man. In Montevideo, he subsisted as a salesman of foreign goods but enjoyed teaching mathematics as a sideline. Giuseppe and Anita were finally married on March 26, 1842. His family moved into a three-room flat at 14 Calle del Porton where three more children were born in a period of seven years. However, civilian life did not suit Garibaldi and he was anxious to answer the call to hardship and glory.

Uruguay at that time was experiencing the grave consequences of a civil war between two factions. One, known as the " Unitarians," was led by Fructuoso Rivera and believed in a strong central government. The other, led by Manuel Oribe, was known as the " Federalists" and believed in relatively loose associations of autonomous provinces. In 1838, Rivera had succeeded in driving Oribe from Uruguay. He found sanctuary in Argentina under the protection of the dictator, Rosas, who had his own designs on Uruguay. Under the urgency of Oribe and the approval of Rosas, military action proceeded against Uruguay. The Great War was to last to 1851.

At first, the Unitarians held their own with induced revolts in Argentina and the support of the French navy. But, in due time, the Argentines came to terms with the diplomatic tenets of the French and were free to expand their naval force under the direction of British Admiral William Brown. In a very short time, Montevideo, as well as the western province of Corrientes, was under siege. Uruguay needed a naval force to bring relief to Corrientes as well as gain some propagandistic value. It could be described as a suicidal mission. The expedition was to sail up the Paraná river through enemy territory for a distance of five hundred miles, at a time of the year when the waters were treacherously low. The leadership of the incursion was to be entrusted to a man who was slowly getting a reputation as a fighter for freedom and disregarded any danger—namely, Giuseppe Garibaldi.

The small fleet consisted of the *Constitucion*, commanded by Garibaldi, the *Pereyra*, *Procida*, and three hundred men. The flotilla set sail from Montevideo on 27 June 1842 for the fortress of Martin Garcia which blocked their passage up the Paraná River. These batteries were on a small island at the junction of the Paraná River and the Uruguay river and proved to be a formidable obstacle. Garibaldi rushed past the fortress at the risk of an intense barrage that produced many dead and wounded but succeeded in getting all ships into the Paraná River. However, after a short distance, the *Constitucion* went aground at the beginning of low tide. Vulnerable and at peril, the men started to transfer the heavy cannon to the smaller transport ship, the *Procida*, but, to their horror, an enemy fleet of seven ships appeared on the horizon heading for them under full sail. Garibaldi, as he revealed in his memoirs, was never to know another predicament in his extraordinary life to be so life threatening. He was never afraid to face death, but he was embarrassed to find himself in such a helpless position. His main cannon was immobilized and the ships were sitting ducks before the ominous power of the Argentine navy. Providence interceded again as the flagship of the enemy also bogged down in the sand. The accompanying enemy ships lost their daring for battle once the leadership had run aground and failed to grasp the initiative. This gave Garibaldi's crew time to free the *Constitucion* and remount her cannon. As if this wasn't enough good fortune, a dense fog settled over the area and provided a perfect cover for the ships to elude the opposing forces and slip up the Paraná River out of harm's way.

The expeditionary force continued up the Paraná River, bypassing offshore batteries with little damage. They were less fortunate when they ventured ashore in attempts for water and food. Furthermore, as they sailed deeper into Corrientes province, the waters became more treacherous and were uncharted. Garibaldi had never been in this area and was at a loss for a pilot to lead him the last few miles through this tortuous and shallow waterway. A seaman was found who was familiar with the area, but he was reluctant to forward any information and prolong what he seemed to be a hopeless cause. A menacing saber to the seamen's throat by Garibaldi persuaded him to facilitate the passage. Navigation was extremely difficult despite the assistance. It took nineteen days to negotiate the shallow waters between El Cerrito and Costa Brava, a distance short of eighty miles.

Passage up the Paraná River ceased at Costa Brava because the water level was now less than seven feet. There, they were met by the friendly fleet from Corrientes, commanded by Lieutenant Villegas. It consisted of one launch with sails and two with oars, hardly an armada. Garibaldi grouped the ships together on the left bank and used cable to bind them into one floating fortress. Those who were not needed to man the cannon were sent ashore under the leadership of Lt. Rodriguez to fend off any land attack. Then, they waited for the pursuing enemy forces.

The Argentine fleet arrived on 14 August under the direction of Admiral Brown. On the fifteenth, enemy troops put ashore and tried to flank Garibaldi from the river bank but were pushed back by Lt. Rodriguez's forces. A violent and savage battle lasted the entire day only to diminish and finally cease at nightfall. During the night, the enemy ships encroached upon the Uruguayans' position. The dawn of Tuesday August 16 must have been a threatening sight to the fighting men of Uruguay. Facing them at a distance of twelve hundred feet sat the Argentine fleet consisting of three brigs, four schooners, three smaller ships, and fifty-three long-range cannons manned by a force of seven hundred experienced fighting men. Garibaldi had six small ships, twenty-three cannons, and three hundred men, in all.

The superiority of the Argentines' artillery proved to be disastrous for the Uruguayans. They immediately were hit by a barrage that took an enormous toll on lives and material. As the day played out, the dead and wounded piled up on the bombed decks; the pumps were in continuous operation to keep the ships afloat. It was an impromptu visit to Pandemonium with the thunderous explosions, the terrifying screams, the incessant maiming, the loss of life everywhere. Finally, night descended on the wholesale destruction and a lull in hostilities pervaded both sides.

During the night, Garibaldi and crew engaged in an ingenious attempt to cause damage to the opposition. Small skiffs were loaded with explosives, torched and aimed downstream in hopes they would hit a vital target. Unfortunately, the Argentine crew deftly maneuvered the floating bombs out of harm's way. The Uruguayan force was demoralized and exhausted; the outcome of this encounter seemed grave for them. During the night, the small Corrientes flotilla slipped away, leaving the remaining Uruguayans to fend for themselves. Garibaldi was furious; he never received desertion very well.

The silence of the dawn of the seventeenth was brutally interrupted by a heavy bombardment that was more incessant than the day before. The Uruguayans were running out of gunpowder and ineffectually tried to use links of chain as projectiles. The situation seemed hopeless and Garibaldi made plans to retreat. The wounded were loaded on small launches and taken ashore. The ships were laced with incendiary spirits and put afire as the remaining crew, with Garibaldi, made a desperate run for it. Unfortunately, the Argentines followed their every movement and pursued with the luxury of greater manpower. As they closed on the retreating forces, the torched ships began exploding with great impact and ending in a deafening, violent explosion when the powder magazine exploded. The pursuing infantry stopped in their tracks wondering from where all the firepower was coming. This allowed Garibaldi and his men enough of a diversion to safely escape into the jungle. Thankfully, the Argentines opted not to pursue. They were assured that they had won the battle.

Admiral Brown had indeed won a military victory, but the small Uruguayan force had gained a moral victory proving that Argentine power could be challenged. But this lost all its value when Rivera's army was destroyed by Oribe on December 6, 1842 at Arroyo Grande. Of this momentous defeat, Dennis Mack Smith wrote in his biography of Garibaldi, "Private ambitions and rivalries in the government were again a contributory cause of this defeat, and Garibaldi had one more lesson here, if only he could have learned from it, that this sort of war rarely settled anything worth settling. Certainly he began now to develop a lifelong distrust of politicians." Corrientes, today, is a province of Argentina.

The city of Montevideo was now exposed to the amassing forces of Oribe under the direction and support of Argentina.

CHAPTER VI: MONTEVIDEO

Montevideo was under siege, but the citizens had no desire to surrender to the hated Argentinians. General Paz was selected to organize the defenses of the city and immediately began to build a series of fortifications and batteries on the periphery of the city. Hurriedly, he recruited local gauchos and molded them into a cavalry as well as reorganized the infantry. Many of the surviving forces were scattered throughout the countryside and slowly filtered back into their units. Munitions, cannon, and armaments were procured by the most clandestine means. Garibaldi was ordered to form another fleet.

The enemy forces slowly but surely assembled on the high ground around Montevideo. The inhabitants of the city feared an attack was imminent when Oribe reached the gates of the city with an army of fourteen thousand men on 16 February 1843. Despite this impending doom, the foreign residents of Montevideo wanted to take an integral part in the defense of their adopted homeland. The French community formed a force of 2,500 men; the Spanish formed a small force that switched sides in a few months; the Italians amassed a legion of five hundred men under Colonel Mancini. Though the Italian Legion was not commanded by Garibaldi, he belonged to the founding committee.

Early skirmishes by the legion were disastrous and the men received unfavorable ethnic slurs as to their fighting ability. Garibaldi took command personally and molded the legion with his "fighting" sailors into an international brigade that was to be hereafter known as the *Garibaldini*. The famous red shirts were also introduced at this time. Garibaldi wanted to dress up his men, who were comprised of a myriad of individualists in different forms of attire—a true ragtag outfit. Unfortunately, the legion's resources were meager and no money could be diverted to uniforms. Through devious means, bundles of red fabric intended to make butchers' smocks were acquired. With the efforts of local seamstresses, the red fabric was custom-made into tunics, which gave the legion some respectability. Hence, the "Red Shirts" of the *Garibaldini*.

Oribe, in the meantime, had tightened his grip on the city and manned all the key positions in the surrounding hills. One of these positions was at El Cerrito, a small hill that was encircled by a ditch that served as a trench. A small house in front of this trench controlled the immediate area. Garibaldi assembled his legion and prepared to attack this position with a bayonet charge, a method of military advancement that would label the *Garibaldini* for years to come. Bayonets glistening in the sunlight and heads lowered, they stubbornly moved forward against a constant hail of bullets. Against the firepower of the mid-nineteenth century, this proved effective despite obvious casualties. The legion succeeded in taking their objective and won the day. The Italian Legion's prowess as a fighting unit was redeemed; no one ever again questioned their courage or fighting ability.

Garibaldi, however, was far from satisfied. Internal discord was rampant and the legion needed to be reorganized and streamlined. With the agreement of the committee, Garibaldi appointed the undertaking to a close friend, Francesco Anzani. Anzani was born in northern Italy on 11 November 1809 and was accomplished in his career as a mercenary. He promptly dismissed incompetent officers and disciplined the men to the ways of the military. He even played an integral part in the final shaping of the red-shirt uniforms. Garibaldi and Anzani had a fervent desire to make the Italian Legion a well-conditioned and precise military force. Their ultimate purpose was to preserve the legion after hostilities had subsided and return to liberate their homeland.

The navies of France and England, in an effort to protect their economic interests, blockaded Montevideo and drove the

Argentinian navy from the port. This fait accompli gave the Uruguayans renewed life and vigor. Garibaldi, with seven hundred legionnaires, embarked upon a small flotilla and ventured up the Uruguay River. They met very little resistance as they sailed up the river toward Salto, where they routed the enemy. However, on 6 December 1845, an Argentine force of 3,500 cavalry, eight hundred infantry, and a battery of field artillery arrived at Salto. Garibaldi's men dug in every hidden area of the village and awaited the attack. The opposing forces were surprised by the concentrated fire of the *Garibaldini* and were driven back. As they were retreating, Garibaldi gave the order for his infamous bayonet charge and drove the enemy from the village.

On February 7, word was received from Rivera that the vanguard of his army under the leadership of Medina was marching toward Salto. The next day, Garibaldi, with 186 cavalrymen and one hundred legionnaires, set out to link up with this detachment. After a few hours out, they were put upon by 1,200 Argentinians and were forced to take refuge in a ruined farmhouse nearby. The enemy closed in on their position, only to be repelled when they were within thirty yards. The concentrated fire wreaked havoc and, again, Garibaldi ordered a bayonet charge and fierce hand-to-hand combat secured their position. However, during the counter charge, the cavalry under the leadership of Baez withdrew to Salto, leaving the *Garibaldini* to their fate.

Garibaldi ordered the forming of a barricade from horse carcasses and human corpses and awaited the next Argentinian wave. An envoy came forward to demand their immediate surrender but received an indignant refusal. The hostilities resumed and the maiming and the killing continued. After nine hours of fighting, Garibaldi realized the position was hopeless and decided to retreat. However, they were surrounded. Their only chance was to crawl a distance of eight hundred yards over open ground to the river where the rich vegetation would offer some cover. At nine P.M., they inched toward the river, warding off the fire of the infantry as well as attacks by the cavalry. At the last moment, Anzani appeared with reinforcements after it was reported to him that Garibaldi's cavalry had deserted. With the added firepower, the *Garibaldini* successfully disengaged themselves from the enemy and limped back to Salto. Garibaldi lost forty-three men and fifty-three were wounded; Argentine total causalities were five hundred dead and wounded. The vanguard of the Uruguayan army reached Salto later that night and the opposing forces left the area.

While this was happening, there was a coup d' etat in Montevideo and the leadership had changed once again, to the chagrin of Garibaldi. Politics had again nullified the noble sacrifice of so many gallant young men. It took three months for the political atmosphere to stabilize and Rivera regained control. He appointed his friends to high positions, diplomatic and military. Garibaldi and his Italian Legion were excluded from any position or compensation for their efforts. In fact, Garibaldi, as a foreigner, was ostracized by the Uruguayan military leaders who selfishly protected their lofty positions. He also was not popular with the business community; the merchants complained to the government whenever he impounded goods to feed his legion. The European diplomats, trying to establish some form of peace in the area, decided that hostilities were inflamed by rival factions and considered the Italian Legion as one of those factions fomenting unrest. It was time for Garibaldi and the *Garibaldini* to look to Italy; their services were no longer essential to Uruguay.

CHAPTER VII: RETURN TO ITALY

Garibaldi had maintained correspondence with Mazzini through the years and knew the time was fertile for revolution in Italy. His father had died, but his mother was still living in Nice and informed Giuseppe of the present political trends. Many Italian exiles arriving in Montevideo brought him up to date as to the republican mood of the country. The Pope (Pius IX), rulers of Naples, Tuscany, and Piedmont, in unprecedented liberal offerings, were magnanimous in granting constitutional and economic reforms. Austria had broken into open revolt; Metternich had resigned and fled to England. Charles Albert had come to the assistance of the provisional government of Milan to drive the Austrians from Lombardy. All this rekindled Garibaldi's passion for a free Italy. He even went as far as to write to Pope Pius IX and offered the services of himself and his legion. He never received an answer. Not to be dissuaded, he made plans to return to Italy with his small band of Redshirts and be available for any opportune event to enhance liberty and freedom in his homeland.

On December 27, 1847, Garibaldi sent his family off to Genoa with a final destination of Nice. Accompanying Anita were their three children—Menotti, Teresita, Ricciotti (nine months old), and the remains of a dead daughter, Rosita. Giacomo Medici was sent ahead to Tuscany on 2 February 1848 to link up with friendly compatriots and await the *Garibaldini*. Anzani had written his brother to liquidate his holdings near Como in hopes of financing the expedition. He was gravely ill (tuberculosis) and desperately wanted to see his homeland once more before he died.

In April 1848, a brig named *Speranza*, sailed out of

Montevideo with seventy-three smiling men aboard. Among them were Anzani, Sacchi, Culiolo, and Minuto, as well as Garibaldi. Most conspicuous was Andres Aguyar, nicknamed "Garibaldi's Moor," a huge Montevidean negro who would save his general's life on many occasions but would die beneath the walls of Rome. These seventy-three hoped to be the birth of a new spirit of liberty and freedom for a unified Italy.

Little did they know that aboard was the true messiah and driving force for a sustained effort to drive the foreigners from Italy. A noble leader, who was to make his mark in history, was being delivered to a noble cause. A rare leader that would inspire the capacity of ordinary individuals to move, act, and mobilize so that they would work together in pursuit of a common end.

During the long two month voyage, Garibaldi had time to think and formulated his plan for a successful effort to unify Italy. With Mazzini, he had professed a desire for a republic state for the people, with elected officials governed by parliamentary law. But the people, Mazzini, and the republicans had a shallow base for such a huge undertaking; it just wasn't practical. They did not have the established armies, nor did they have the diplomatic ties to keep the European powers from interfering. They didn't have funds to acquire munitions, cannon, and rifles, or to maintain logistics. On the other hand, the monarchy of Piedmont was favorable toward an united Italy and possessed the necessary means to launch the initial effort. They had an established army as well as resources to sustain a prolonged military campaign. They had a recognized diplomatic corps and governmental ties throughout Europe. In his final analysis, Garibaldi did not agree with a monarchist government for his beloved Italy, but realized that the only way to achieve preliminary freedom was to use the forces of Piedmont. Once Italy was united, he thought, time would decide the fate of the monarchy.

As soon as the ship was in the deep blue waters of the Mediterranean, Garibaldi knew he was home. Nowhere in the world was the sea this characteristic deep blue. Anita was expecting him at Nice, and Mazzini and the Republicans were awaiting him at Genoa where he landed on 28 June 1848, to a tumultuous display of admiration. The escapades of the Redshirts had preceded them and been embellished by the press to a point that the local adoration of the infamous Italian Legion was a growing frenzy. However, they hardly looked like the saviors of Italy. After two months on the open sea, they resembled hoodlums ready to usurp some unduly right to an undeserved position. Dressed in tattered clothes, with unmatched colors and mismatched insignias, with unkempt beards and shoulder-length hair, the *Garibaldini* seemed more like brigands rather than the salvation of a free Italy. However, no one noticed the rifles that they slung so lackadaisically on their shoulders were field clean and in perfect working order.

Emboldened by this reception, Garibaldi went directly to the king of Piedmont, Charles Albert, to offer his services. He got a chilly reception. Slightly disappointed, he returned to Nice where he received a passionate reception that buoyed his mood. He finally was reunited with his mother and family. During the following months, he went back and forth from Genoa to Torino, the capital of Piedmont, from one ministry to another, with no encouragement from those in control.

King Charles Albert, Piedmont's ruler, was hesitant to give Garibaldi any military power, fearing his reverence by the people. The generals in command looked down in contempt on this untrained upstart and his gang of bedraggled insurgents from South America. Eventually, the *Garibaldini* marched on to Milan in Lombardy and received a favorable response from the provisional government. Garibaldi was requested to amass a volunteer corps around the nucleus of his Italian Legion and assist in the war against the Austrians. With the assistance of Medici and Sacchi (Anzani had died on July 4), he succeeded in forming a legion of five thousand and marched on to Lake Como. Once at Como, word reached them that the Piedmont army had been handily beaten at Custoza and Charles Albert had quit the war to free Lombardy.

The vast majority of Garibaldi's volunteers deserted and returned to their homes. Charles Albert ordered Garibaldi to cease all hostilities. Garibaldi refused and continued operations. He claimed his right as a free citizen to continue the fight alone; he was, after all, under commission of Milan and not Piedmont. Charles Albert issued an order for Garibaldi's arrest. He defied the king's order for his arrest and, under the doctrine of popular insurrection, he called upon the people to take up a scythe or even a stick to carry the cause of an independent Italy forward. Again, Garibaldi was affected by political forces around him and was left to his own fate.

Undaunted, with a force of one thousand and urging others to join, he pushed on to Lake Maggiore to confront the Austrian army. In a series of small battles, the *Garibaldini* showed formidable talent in upsetting the normal affairs of the Austrian held countryside. More than anything, Garibaldi revealed exceptional skill in fighting "South America" style with such a small force. Using surprise as their most effective weapon, being mobile, and never confronting the enemy head on when odds were greatly against them, proved to be a disrupting influence to the Austrian forces. Guerrilla warfare was indeed born and active in the nineteenth century. The escapades of Garibaldi and the Italian Legion were soon revered throughout Europe.

However, Garibaldi and a dwindling force of five hundred men were completely encircled on August 26, 1848 by five thousand Austrians at Morazzone. The *Garibaldini* fought bravely the entire day to withstand the constant barrage of such superior forces, but something dramatic and heroic had to be done to avoid the inevitable. During that night, Garibaldi led a bayonet charge and succeeded in breaking through the Austrian lines and opened an escape route. Once out of danger, the legion dispersed and went their separate ways. The Lombardy campaign was finished.

Garibaldi was in ill health (malaria) and full of despair as he made his way back to Nice. He was extremely disappointed in the common people and their inability to rally for the cause of nationalism. He wrote, "All the weaknesses of our character had been revealed . . . the results of our rhetorical education and our soft and antimilitary way of life."

He continued to speak forcefully for independence in Nice, San Remo, and Genoa. Being an effective and passionate speaker with a panache for the altruistic, he was adored as an honest leader who was sincere in his convictions for a free Italy. In October 1848, he was elected one of the Ligurian deputies to the parliament at Torino. As he despised politics, he never assumed that seat, but rather took to rallying his countryman to thoughts of independence. Subsequently, the *Garibaldini* headed for Bologna to assist in leading a force against Austria in the liberation of Venice. The provisional government of Bologna wanted no part of these reactionaries. They had no choice but to spend the winter in the Apennines among a hostile population, at a loss for food and shelter. It was at this time that the state of affairs changed dramatically in Rome and for Garibaldi.

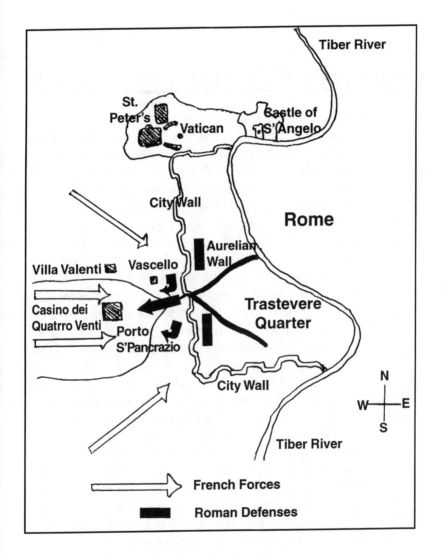

Defense of Rome 1849

CHAPTER VIII: ROMAN CAMPAIGN OF 1849

Pope Pius IX had succeeded in angering the masses with his failure to support the war against the Austrians. He tried to appease the populace by appointing Pelligrino Rossi, a Tuscan, to the head of the government. Rossi, in his conservative and rigid subjugation, was unable to quell the ugly mood of the Romans. On 15 November 1848, Rossi was surrounded by sixty angry veterans of the war with raised weapons. When they withdrew, Pelligrino Rossi lay dead at their feet. News of the assassination triggered a series of riots and street demonstrations, which became more inflamed with each passing day. The Pope, fearing for his life, on 24 November fled to Gaeta under the protection of Ferdinand II of Naples. Rome was in a state of anarchy and a prime target for overthrow by subversive forces.

The Republican Committee of Mazzini set up a provisional government and sent a national call for volunteers as well as the *Garibaldini*. As aforementioned, Garibaldi was in winter quarters in the Apennines suffering the rigors of a cold mountainous terrain and a sometimes hostile population when he received the Roman call to arms. He immediately ordered a march south in hope this was the historic spark to spread the fire of liberation for a united Italy. Surprisingly, each town they passed was more friendly than the next; the tide of popular support was swinging in their favor. In Ravenna and Bologna, after being rejected just a few months before, his forces swelled with the enlistment of volunteers destined to have an important role in the coming battles for the defense of Rome. Medici, Bixio, Masina, Bassi, and others now became an integral part of Garibaldi's high command.

The *Garibaldini* arrived at Rieti, a valley town outside of Rome, in January 1849. There, they regrouped. New uniforms were issued—dark blue coats with green collars, dark blue trousers with green stripes, and Calabrian hats with red bands. The officers retained their South American dress with identifiable ostrich plumes in their caps. Garibaldi had changed his striped poncho for a white one. The *Garibaldini* were primped to take their place in Italian history.

When the famed *Garibaldini* entered Rome via the Corso toward the Piazza Colonna, thousands greeted them as they made their way through the ancient Roman ruins under an aura of a new historic beginning for the Italian people. Drums rolled, trumpets blared, and Garibaldi led his legion, elegantly attired in his South American poncho and a feathered cap; his white stallion cantered slowly through the mass of admirers. Many international artists were moved that day to capture the magnanimity of that historic scene. The Romans burst with pride as Italian partisans marched forward to claim Italy for all Italians after centuries of bondage. Garibaldi regaled on all this adulation, but was quite aware that the battle to bring all this to fruition was ahead. Foreign powers were not readily amenable to an Italian Republic at the expense of the papacy, especially the French and her new president, Louis-Napoleon, nephew of Emperor Bonaparte.

In March 1849, Mazzini was elected to a triumvirate with Aurelio Saffi and Carlo Armellini to govern Rome, but Mazzini assumed charge and, in effect, controlled Rome. Garibaldi was elected deputy from Rieti to the National Assembly. Against the advice of some perverse Roman leaders, the Minister of War, Avezanna, designated Garibaldi a general with extraordinary military power, his prowess as a martial genius preceding him. Garibaldi desired to be commander-in-chief, but accepted the role beneath General Roselli, whom he regarded as an inferior rather than be lost in political infighting.

Unexpectedly, on 25 April 1849, the French fleet sailed in to Roman territory with a detachment of French soldiers with the purpose of restoring the Pope. The National Assembly desired to appease the French, who contested the Italianization of the papacy. The triumvirs were bitterly embroiled in debate as to the next course of action. Garibaldi, adamantly opposed to appeasement, wanted to drive the French from Italian soil. Mazzini, on the other hand, was more moderate and wanted to set up some middle ground with the great power. The Assembly, under much chafing histrionics, voted to resist. They cried, "Viva l'Italie."

In the beginning, Garibaldi defended the east from the Neapolitans, suspecting the Pope would use this opportunity to stir Ferdinand II into action. When the French landed at Civita Vecchia with a force of ten thousand, Garibaldi was hurriedly brought to the gates of Rome. With a force of only 2,300, he defended the Porte San Pancrazio and Porte Caveleggia, as well as the gardens of the Vatican. The French were beaten back. Garibaldi made the request for fresh troops to administer the coup de grace to the retreating French troops. Mazzini interceded and denied the request, fearing a complete annihilation of the French would send ominous reverberations throughout Europe. Garibaldi proceeded alone with his tired and haggard legion in anticipation that Roman reinforcements would rally to his position.

He pursued the enemy and was finally approached by a French officer wishing to declare an armistice on May 1, 1849, which was granted. At the same time, an order came from Mazzini that he and his men return to Rome. Garibaldi and his legion returned to Rome among a tumultuous roar from the populace; the star of Garibaldi had ascended. The Romans turned to the wounded, French and Republican alike. Many women offered their services at various hospitals. Among these was Anita, who had joined her husband after daringly crossing the French and Austrian lines with eight-year-old Menotti.

The Roman clergy, meanwhile, were busy organizing bands of papist partisans known as *Sanfedisti*, who displayed their ferocity in neighboring small towns and villages. They swore, "... hatred for all enemies of our one, true, holy Roman Catholic religion." Many Republicans were killed by terrorist activities of the *Sanfedisti* in the name of religion. However, neither side was innocent of atrocities as indiscreet passion was ubiquitous.

On May 1, the Neapolitan army was advancing from the south with a force of twenty thousand men and thirty-six cannons. Garibaldi, with a force of 2,700 men, intercepted them on May 8 and defeated them at Velletri. The Neapolitans were awed by his invincibility. They did not care to test his aura of immortality and broke ranks as they fled south. Garibaldi was hurriedly brought back to Rome on the twelfth of May, after word was received that a Spanish force had landed on the southern shore and was marching on Rome. The Austrians, with a force of twenty thousand, had taken Ferrara and Bologna and were now marching on Rome. In the meantime, the French had increased their position to thirty thousand men, forty cannons, forty-eight artillery pieces, and various howitzers and mortars. The noose was indeed tightening around the Roman Republic.

On May 19, the Neapolitans were again marching north but with their king, Ferdinand II, at the head to give his troops fervor and determination against the great Garibaldi. It did them little good, as the *Garibaldini* met them and beat them into submission. The fighting was intense but, in the end, the Neapolitans retreated to Velletri. The *Garibaldini* limped back to Rome on May 31, exhausted but firm in their determination to fight for their new republic.

The original armistice (May 1) with the French was to extend to June 4, but the French unexpectedly attacked at three A.M. on June 3. The republican forces and the *Garibaldini* were in disarray and turmoil. Officers and their units were separated and mass confusion was everywhere. Intense fighting broke out all over Rome, especially at the Casino dei Quattro Venti. Garibaldi needed more time to assemble his officers scattered about the city. Suicidal bayonet charges did little to break the siege. Many of Rome's bravest died that day. Garibaldi's division alone lost one thousand, among them was Garibaldi's South American lieutenant, Andres Aguyar. The odds were hopelessly against the Republicans, outnumbered and ill-trained compared to the disciplined French. They were now losing the passionate embrace of the Romans as the tide of the war was shifted.

The next day, June 4, the French set their artillery on the newly gained positions and unmercifully bombarded the city for weeks. Many priceless works of art were lost forever; the area of

Trastevere was almost obliterated from the earth. The ceaseless bombardment and the incessant fire from snipers produced scores of dead and injured. Intermittent truces were called to allow the populace to clear the carnage. For a month, the Republican forces held out with the infectious self-confidence of their leader. But on June 30, wearied, injured, and his uniform in shreds, Garibaldi spoke before the National Assembly and dejectedly admitted that the defense of Rome was no longer possible. He pleaded, ". . . the remnants of the Republican forces must live to fight another day and the young, brave freedom-fighters shall have the opportunity to etch their names in history. Then, and only then, shall Italy gain its proper status among nations."

On July 2, Garibaldi, with Anita, spoke to his followers at the magnificent piazza in front of St. Peter's. He said, "Fortune, which today has betrayed us, will smile on us tomorrow. I am leaving Rome. Whoever wishes to continue the war against the foreigner, let him come with me. I offer neither pay nor quarters nor provisions. I offer hunger, thirst, forced marches, battles, and death." Leaving behind 3,500 dead and wounded, four thousand men began their slow procession out of Rome. They planned to continue the fight in the mountains and marshes of central Italy, maybe finding refuge in San Marino. Then, when the situation was right, the attack on Rome would be resumed. However, Garibaldi's stock deteriorated overnight. At Tivoli the next morning, desertions had decreased the four thousand to twenty-five hundred, including many officers who had fought with him in South America. Many of these deserters raided monasteries and villages for food and loot and incensed the people of the region. Consequently, villages barred their gates to the retreating forces. They gave no support to the revolution.

This made a despondent Garibaldi write, "How you must despise this hermaphrodite generation of Italians, these countrymen of mine whom I often tried to ennoble, little though they deserve it. The fact is that treachery has paralyzed every generous movement. We have been dishonored, and the name of Italian will be a laughing stock for foreigners in every country. I am disgusted to belong to a family of so many cowards."

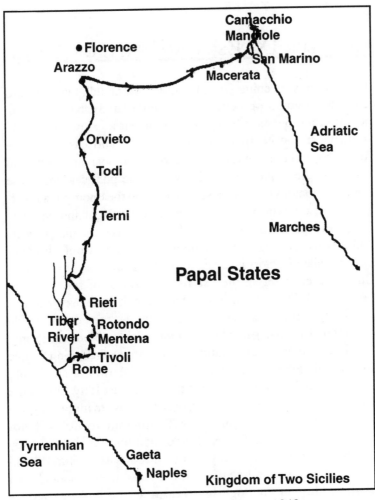

Garibaldi's Retreat from Rome, 1849.

CHAPTER IX: ESCAPE/DEATH OF ANITA

The very next evening, Tuesday July 3, Garibaldi, his men, and Anita departed the peaceful gardens and palatial estate of Tivioli, hopeful their pursuers had given up the chase. However, to the south were the Neapolitans, to the north and east were the Austrians, and to the west were six thousand Spaniards, who had landed at the request of the Holy See, the political arm of the Pope. Garibaldi's only purpose was to elude the enemy at all costs and to preserve the remainder of his forces to fight another day.

After a day's march, he consulted with his remaining officers and a consensus agreed that their only refuge would be with Daniele Manin, who was still resisting the Austrian siege in Venice. But the men, after all their sacrifices and loss of friends, were becoming disillusioned in a way that made them unacceptable as a fighting unit. This was in strong contrast to the worldwide reputation they had gained in their formidable defense of Rome.

That evening they set northward in hope of reaching Venice by way of temporary sanctuary in San Marino, a small, old republic that had remained neutral in northeast Italy. Discipline was deteriorating with each day, desertions were increasing at a rapid rate and the populace was reluctant to help, if not downright hostile to Garibaldi and his men. On July 8, they reached Terni, where they were united with a Republican regiment of nine hundred under the leadership of Colonel Hugh Forbes. He was an English adventurer who had married an Italian and gotten caught up with the fervor of the revolutionary movement in Venice and Rome, but now he was retreating from the Austrians and on the run. Garibaldi and Forbes were successful in evading the Spaniards, French, and Neapolitans, but they could not shake off the relentless Austrians, who were blocking their progress northward. By many a circuitous routes, they avoided the enemy for days until the rear guard had to defend themselves at Arezzo against the Austrians. The peasants aided the enemy in apprehending stragglers and wounded Republicans. Garibaldi was furious and disgusted with his fellow countrymen and laid this defect in Italian character at the feet of priests and friars. ". . . those ministers of falsehood, the black brood, pestilent scum of humanity, caryatid of thrones still reeking with the scent of human burnt offerings where tyranny still reigns."

Garibaldi, Anita (sick and pregnant), Forbes, Ugo Bassi (priest and patriot), and a combined force of 1,500 entered San Marino on the morning of July 31 with the Austrian pursuers closely on their heels. The governing body of San Marino extended their hospitality to the *Garibaldini*, but the Austrians surrounded the small country (twenty-four square miles) and demanded their expulsion. Garibaldi officially dissolved his force that night and allowed each to fend for himself. He spoke, "We have reached the land of refuge, and we owe the best possible behavior to our generous hosts. We, too, have merited the consideration due to persecuted misfortune. Soldiers, I release you from your duty to follow me and leave you free to return to your homes. But remember that although the Roman war for the independence of Italy has ended, Italy remains in shameful slavery."

Later, speaking to his staff at the western gate, he said, "Whoever wishes to follow me, I offer him fresh battles, suffering, and exile. But treaties with the foreigner, never!" Then, with his usual flair for the dramatic, he leaped on his horse and galloped through the gate. Anita, now with chills and fever, followed, against Garibaldi's wishes. Ugo Bassi, Colonel Forbes, and 250 of his closest followers all joined the general as he made a run for Cesantico, on the Adriatic. They reached the coast the next day, where Garibaldi and a force reduced to 150 seized thirteen small fishing boats and set sail for Venice. On the moonlit night of August 2, a feverish Anita and an exhausted Garibaldi, with their small flotilla, were spotted by the Austrian navy. Most of the boats were apprehended by dawn and all aboard were later imprisoned, including Colonel Forbes. As fate would have it, four boats eluded capture and beached near Magnavacca. Garibaldi, immediately, divided the survivors and sent them in different directions. Then, with his delirious wife in his arms and a close friend, Major Giambattista Culiolo, he ran for the marshes of Comacchio. Most of the other group that had made it to the beach were instantly caught and subsequently shot on the spot, including Ugo Bassi, the cleric of the *Garibaldini*.

Garibaldi, with his delirious wife and Culiolo, who limped terribly from a wound received in Rome, would have fared no better had not a benefactor reached them in the marshes of Comacchio. This man had met Garibaldi eight months before on his march south to Rome at Ravenna. In fact, his brother had been killed in Rome and another had returned with Garibaldi as far as San Marino. His name was Giocchino Bonnet, local landowner who had been frantically searching for the fugitives to assist them in any way. He and a local guide supported the febrile Anita, whose condition was deteriorating with each hour, and dragged her to a hut on the other side of the marsh with the exhausted Garibaldi and the limping Culiolo following close behind. Feverish, convulsive, and delirious, Anita was put to bed; concern was growing for her life. Garibaldi, Anita, and Culiolo rested through the night, only to be abruptly awakened and transported early in the morning to a new hideaway across a lagoon and into a hidden valley. Bonnet protested the transfer of Anita who, in her condition, would be a detriment to the success of the escape, but Garibaldi would have none of it. It was evening when the refugees arrived at Guiccioli's dairy farm near the remote town of Mandriole.

Toward the end of the day's journey, Anita, in a brief moment of lucidity, clutched Giuseppe and murmured, ". . . José, the children . . ." but then went into violent convulsions. At the farmhouse she passed into unconsciousness. Garibaldi held her in his arms and he lovingly wiped foam from her mouth as a local doctor was summoned in a desperate attempt to save her life.

The doctor was aghast at the condition of this twenty-nine-year-old woman, six months pregnant and in the throes of death. He was little solace to Giuseppe, who pleaded for her recovery.

Anita's forced breathing reverberated through the cottage and sounds of her dyspnea produced and aura of death until the early morning hours. Suddenly, the rales stopped and the solemn doctor leaned over his patient. He said, sotto voce, "È Morta." Anita Garibaldi died on Saturday morning of August 4, 1849.

"No! No! No!" screamed Garibaldi. "It cannot be! She is my wife, the mother of my children! She is my life! Anita wake up! Oh, Anita, what have I lost?" Garibaldi went berserk, screaming and sobbing over this cruel twist of fate. He punched the wall with all his might as if to deter the reaper; he kicked over chairs and tables in reaction to this great loss and could not be subdued. He had no time to reflect on this, his reaction was spontaneous, an instinctive response to something totally grotesque and unwelcome in his life. After a time and much anguish, he sheepishly leaned on a door jamb and slowly sunk to the floor, where he wept uncontrollably. He was devastated and alone in an angry world.

At length, he was approached by a teary Major Culiolo, who made him realize the seriousness of their position as well as the constant danger his presence placed on the kind farmhands who had showed him refuge. Too depressed to resist, Garibaldi agreed to leave the hastily interred body of Anita and escape. With the assistance of the doctor's cart and a guide, they received refuge at a cobbler's home in Sant' Alberto, three miles away. At dawn, August 5, Culiolo and Garibaldi raced for the heavy forest north of Ravenna, where they were greeted by many partisans. Moving from house to house and at night, they crossed the Romagna plain to Forli and then over the Apennines into Tuscany. Eventually, on September 2, they reached his father's birthplace at Chiavari, just south of Genoa.

The heroic welcome Garibaldi received in Genoa was an embarrassment to the Piedmont monarchy. Foreign pressures forced King Victor Emmanuel (Charles Albert's son) to rid themselves of this revolutionary. He offered Garibaldi exile rather than imprisonment, hoping the popular leader would eventually lose his popularity in a foreign country. On September 11, Garibaldi agreed to leave Piedmont via Nice to visit his family.

CHAPTER X: EXILE

It was a sad return to Quai Papacino, the dock of his birthplace at the harbor in Nice. A small, quiet crowd had assembled that morning at his family's home, advance news of Anita's death had hit the community like a death knell. His aging mother (seventy-nine) was the first to greet him; she was very frail and showed her years. Once inside, his three children—Menotti, nearly nine; Teresita, four; and Ricciotti, two—were lined up and sobbing, "Where is Momma?" Garibaldi quickly picked up the little girl as the boys clutched his legs and all began crying uncontrollably. The sorrow of that moment was to haunt him for years in his exile. Within twenty-four hours, he left the boys in the care of a cousin and Teresita with the family of Deidris and sailed away aboard the *Tripoli* to begin his exile.

His original place of exile was to be Tunis, but the Bey of Tunis refused to allow him to land in his small country. The ship detoured back across the Mediterranean and dropped Garibaldi off at La Maddalena, a small island off the northern coast of Sardinia. He stayed there for three weeks until he got an invitation from the British Governor of Gibraltar. Once there, he was informed that, although he was welcome in England as a political refugee, he could only stay in Gibraltar not more than fifteen days. He applied for sanctuary in Spain, but was denied. He then was offered a temporary home by the Piedmontese consul at Tangier on the Mediterranean coast of North Africa.

He remained in Tangier for seven months, fishing, hunting and reminiscing of happier days. He was accompanied by his dog and Major Culiolo, who followed the general into exile and supported him as an aide. The Piedmontese consul to Tangier, Giovanni Carpanetti, also joined him occasionally. It was during this time that he began writing his memoirs, expounding on his South American adventures. Garibaldi tried unsuccessfully to resume his merchant marine career, but political pressures were brought upon anyone who dared to employ him. After much apathy and boredom, he decided to go to America. He thought of returning to Montevideo, but negated that upon closer consideration, he didn't want to return to the homeland and memories of his beloved Anita. Instead, on 12 June 1850, he sailed for New York City by way of Liverpool, England.

Seven weeks later, on 29 July 1850, Garibaldi arrived in the harbor of New York City aboard the English ship Waterloo. The magnanimous structure of the Statue of Liberty or the somber Ellis Island had not gained their place in history, as yet. His arrival was well publicized and hordes of enduring enthusiasts met his ship at New York's harbor. Depressed and ailing from recurring rheumatism, he declined all honorary banquets and testimonials in his honor. He was made aware of strong Catholic opposition to any American recognition for him. His anticlerical feelings were well known. At first he moved in with a fellow Italian at Irving Place, but then attained residence in the house of Antonio Meucci at 420 Tomkins Avenue, Staten Island.

Antonio Meucci would gain his own place in history as the controversial inventor of the telephone. There are some Italian-Americans who designate him as the inventor of the telephone; he introduced a caveat to the United States Patent Office for the invention some five years before Alexander Bell made his application. Meucci never patented his invention, but Bell did and the rest is history. Garibaldi was employed in Meucci's candle factory as a tallow-chandler. It was a boring and routine existence to a man who had fended off national armies and loved adventure and action. Melancholic and homesick, his only solace was the company of his fellow Italians and the thought of renewing his effort for national liberty. He continued writing his autobiography, a lengthy discourse on his early years and South American campaigns. After months of ordinary, predictable life, he applied for American citizenship but never completed the formalities to make his naturalization official.

On many occasions, after working long hours at the factory, he would stroll to the harbor. The smell of the open sea and watching crews tend to their ship chores made him ache for the role of ship's captain. He even asked some of the ship owners for a job, but was turned down as his limited English was a handicap. Sullen and depressed, he slowly returned to his home and the candle factory, more unhappy than earlier.

Finally, in the spring of 1851, he joined a friend, Francesco Carponeto, on a business trip to Peru. Garibaldi was elated to be on the open sea once more and relished the chance to see the rest of the world. However, he contracted marsh fever while at Panama and delayed his arrival in Peru until the beginning of October 1851. In Peru he was well received by the Italian community. In the spring of 1852, he became the captain of the *Carmen* through a Genoan benefactor who had made his fortune in Peru. Sailing under the Peruvian flag, he traveled to the Far East visiting the ports of Canton, Hong Kong, Macao, Manila, and returning by way of Australia and New Zealand. In 1853, he left Lima, again on the same ship, and rounded Cape Horn, sailing north across the Atlantic Ocean to New York City.

He languished in the United States for months without anything eventful or memorable recorded. Once more, he was becoming homesick and anxious to be reunited with his family after recently being informed of his mother's death. Foremost in his mind was the continued struggle of a united Italy. He wrote to a friend, Augusto Vecchi, ". . . terrified at the likely prospect of never again wielding a sword in her name. I thought distance could diminish the bitterness in my soul, but unfortunately it is not true, and I have led an unhappy life, restless and embittered by memory. Yes, I am athirst for the emancipation of our country . . . But the Italians of today think of the belly, not of the soul."

In due time, he was awarded the captaincy of a small vessel, the *Commonwealth*, which was bound for England under an American flag but owned by a wealthy Italian from Boston. After a four year absence, he was afforded a tumultuous reception at Newcastle, England, but as in New York, he refused any banquets or public receptions. However, he received a deputation of several miners aboard ship who presented him with a sword and a telescope. Garibaldi replied in his heavily accented English, "As one of the people—a workman like yourselves—I value very highly these expressions of your esteem . . . Italy will one day be a nation, and its free citizens will know how to acknowledge all the kindness shown her exiled sons in the days of her darkest troubles. Should England at any time in a just cause need my arm, I am ready to unsheathe in her defense this noble and splendid sword received at your hands."

But there were others who were anxious to meet with him and it wasn't all tea and sympathy. Mazzini as well as other exiled Republicans were living in London and wanted an immediate discourse with Garibaldi. Mazzini, in particular, valued Garibaldi's name as a symbol of freedom and wanted to use his popularity in a incursion to Sicily, where they were ready for revolt. Garibaldi, on the other hand, had desired to separate his plan for a united Italy with the assistance of the head of the House of Savoy, King Victor Emmanuel from Mazzini and his Republicans. He blamed much of the failure of the Rome campaign on Mazzini.

But more than the parting of the ways of two historic figures, a storm of political intrigue was being played out on the Italian national scene.

CHAPTER XI: RISORGIMENTO/CAPRERA

Italy's heroic efforts from 1848 to 1849 failed for many reasons but mainly because of the insistence of the Austrian government on sending reinforcements in the north and the decision of Louis Napoleon to intervene in the Pope's behalf. Rome and Venice lost their bid for independence in the same year and created a lull in the movement for a united Italy. The only saving grace for the Italians was the liberal constitution of Piedmont-Sardinia granted by King Charles Albert. However, Charles Albert had abdicated in favor of his son, Victor Emmanuel II, after the king's defeat at Novara to the Austrians in March 1849. This began a period of political unity known as the *Risorgimento* (Revival) that laid the groundwork for a later attempt at national unity. Three prominent figures in Italian history were responsible for sustaining this resurgence of political harmony and all were Piedmontese.

The treaty of London (1720) ceded the island of Sardinia to the Royal House of Savoy in Piedmont. Victor Emmanuel, the heir to the House of Savoy and the throne, was twenty-seven when he became king of Piedmont-Sardinia and the chancelleries of Europe expected to take advantage of such a young monarch on a world stage. The new king was both ridiculed and admired. He was ridiculed for his untidy dress and brutish habits; his appetite for women was voracious and untamed. He was hardly the epitome of a regal monarch and was referred to in European courts as the "Royal Buffoon." However, Victor Emmanuel strongly supported the *Risorgimento* and the movement toward Italian national unity; he defended the liberal Constitution from all European challenges. With the assistance of his premiers, d'Azeglio and Cavour, he developed parliamentary government, raised the quality of the army, reorganized finances, encouraged commerce and industry, and transferred ecclesiastical property to civil control. Marchese Massimo d' Azeglio was another important figure in defending the Piedmont-Sardinia Constitution and extolling nationalism. A veteran who survived previous battles for independence and was wounded at Vicenza, he was tapped by his king to head a government. As Piedmont's first prime minister, he was instrumental in the peace talks of 1849 and, from a weak position, wrested a treaty from Austria that was favorable to his king and the Constitution. The Austrian armies were still encamped on Piedmont territory when they demanded a war indemnity of two hundred million francs and the abrogation of the Constitution. Premier d' Azeglio's rebuttal was that the Constitution would never be abolished and the government would pay not a franc more than seventy-five million. Furthermore, he demanded that Austria withdraw their troops from Piedmont as well as grant amnesty to all who participated in the hostilities. Quite a stance by an inexperienced premier whose country had lost a war. But to the surprise of most of the diplomatic corps of Europe, Austria agreed to all terms. Austria had internal problems (Hungary had revolted) and was anxious to disentangle itself from any armed conflict in Italy. Consequently, Piedmont became a beacon to European refugees who were seeking less conservative political systems.

An important figure in d' Azeglio's cabinet, Conte di Camillo Benso Cavour, was adroit at manipulating political action. Born in 1810, he was educated by the parliamentary systems and courts of Europe. The consummate Piedmont politician and Machiavellian, he became, at different times, Minister of Agriculture, of the Navy, and of Finance. Also, he was the cofounder with Cesare Balboa of the newspaper, *Il Risorgimento*, in 1847, which was the voice of the movement for Italian political unification. He became prime minister for the Piedmont-Sardinia monarchy in 1852 and was a revolutionary conspirator posing as a diplomat. He, too, realized Italy's chance for unification lie in the assistance of at least one of the great powers.

His foreign policies revolved around alliances with England and France; Austria remained the main obstacle to a free Italy. Although Garibaldi and he did not agree on many items (Garibaldi loathed politicians), Premier Cavour was to become the political architect of national unification from 1852 until his death in 1861.

Meanwhile, Garibaldi, with the approval of the Piedmont government, left England and continued to Genoa aboard the *Commonwealth* and finally was reunited with his family at Nice in May 1954. He was to stay in Nice for over a year and captained occasional charters to local ports in the Mediterranean. Although he saw his children more than he had in the last four years, they were separated from him. Menotti, fourteen, was attending a military college. Teresita, ten, was still with the family Deidris. Ricciotti, eight, was in England recovering from medical treatment and stayed with guardians. Garibaldi aspired to acquire a residence of his own that the children and he could call home; he wanted so badly to create a home nest.

On one of his commercial voyages, he was forced, because of a violent storm, to take refuge in the waters off the island of Maddelena, just north of Sardinia. It was here that he discovered a small island adjacent to Maddelena and was touched by its natural splendor and remoteness. Caprera was four miles by three, windy, hilly, rocky, barren, and overgrown with underbrush, but Garibaldi fell in love with the small island and was determined to acquire it for his home. Through the inheritance from his brother, Felice, and other benefactors, he purchased half of the island (Garibaldi acquired the other half in later years). He moved onto this "mass of granite" in November 1855, his only shelter being a sail spread out like a tent, which was frequently carried away by the fierce, constant winds.

A small wooden house was built the first year mainly for the comfort of his daughter, Teresita. A larger stone house was added, in South America style, and completed late in 1857. At his new home, Garibaldi labored as a farmer, home builder, herder, and family patriarch. The island was resistant to bountiful crop yields partly due to infertile soil, but mostly due to Garibaldi's inexperience as a farmer. No natural harbor existed to the island, but the reefs nearby provided outstanding fishing. The family, in the beginning, was subjected to a constant diet of fish. The livestock, primarily made up of goats and cattle, roamed freely on the island and trampled crops and fences alike. Garibaldi named each one and treated them as pets; he allowed no one to discipline them. He was at peace during those laborious years, rearing his family and distancing himself from the political scene. However, he frequently had guests from the mainland and kept his ear attuned to the growing restlessness for a united Italy.

Garibaldi was summoned to Turin in August 1856 and met Cavour for the first time. It was a strained meeting, but the two men tried to be cordial to one another. However, Cavour tried to impress on Garibaldi that heroic plans were in the making for a free Italy. He wanted to keep the general in check and inactive, as Mazzini had embarrassed the Piedmont government by his disastrous insurrections in Lombardy. Garibaldi was recalled to Turin in August 1858 and again heard much rhetoric about future plans for war with Austria. It was on this occasion that he met with the king and a bond was created between the two that lasted for years. From that moment, Garibaldi wanted Victor Emmanuel proclaimed as unlimited military dictator to dissuade idle chatter and squabbles of parliament and politicians. Cavour resisted this movement, which would weaken his position and thus began a rift between the two.

Garibaldi was not sent for again by the government until February 1859. He knew that this request was more urgent than the rest; his agents in Turin had been informed. A new dawn was to begin for a united Italy as well as the realization of the destiny of one of Italy's greatest warriors—Giuseppe Garibaldi.

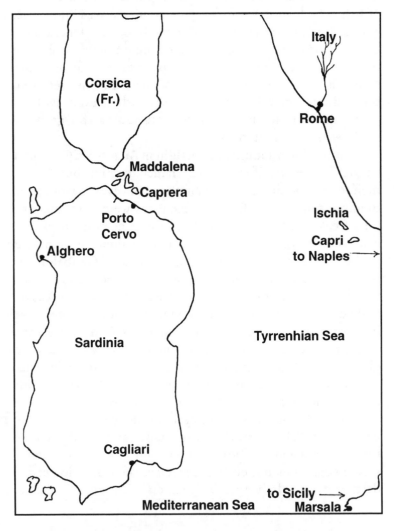

Caprera - Garibaldi's Home for Twenty-Six Years

CHAPTER XII: CACCIATORI DELLE ALPI

As Garibaldi sailed across the Mediterranean that cold January, his thoughts went back eleven years to when he returned from South America. Now, he was more than ever convinced about an alliance with the Piedmont government and its king. The Republicans of Mazzini were ineffective in their attempts at insurrection and now were divisive in their approach. He had reinforced the idea of having a royal dictatorship bestowed upon Victor Emmanuel. He believed it would give him greater access to the king's military resources and keep meddling politicians at bay.

Cavour had aligned himself with Emperor Napoleon III of France. (Louis-Napoleon had himself crowned in December 1852). When Britain and France went to war with Russia, Piedmont, in the spring of 1855, sent eighteen thousand troops to the Crimea at the insistence of Napoleon III. After cessation of hostilities in 1856, Cavour sat at the side of the victors at the Congress of Paris. He attempted to interject the Italian question at the meeting, but Austria would have none of it. However, he impressed on Louis-Napoleon the importance of gaining leadership in Europe from Austria. In January 1859, France and Piedmont completed a military treaty which stated that if there was an Austrian attack on Piedmont forces, France would come to the aid of Piedmont to rid the Austrian forces from the Lombardo-Veneto sector, once and for all.

Shortly after the treaty was signed and the invitation granted to Garibaldi, thousands of volunteers streamed into Piedmont from all over the peninsula, anxious to do battle with Austria. Austria issued an ultimatum on 23 April to Piedmont; it was to demobilize and disperse the volunteers within three days. Victor

Emmanuel and Cavour refused and war was declared.

Cavour thought Garibaldi to be nothing but a rabble rouser and short on intellectual capabilities, but he needed to control the massive popular support of this national hero in the imminent war with Austria. Garibaldi, on the other hand, had little in common with this aristocratic, pompous, double-dealing politician but was anxious to unsheathe his sword in the honor of his homeland and to serve his king. To the surprise of a few, Garibaldi was appointed in charge of the *Cacciatori delle Alpi* (Alpine chausseurs), a completely volunteer corps designed to muffle his military talents.

Garibaldi was enthusiastic to have the opportunity to return to military command despite many restrictions put upon his volunteer force. It was not to include more than three thousand men, nor was it to include any cavalry or artillery. There were innumerable frustrations over supplies and much dissatisfaction with the poor quality of men. The corps was only assigned those volunteers who were not wanted elsewhere; this proved to be a serious restraint as volunteers were streaming into Piedmont to join Garibaldi. General La Marmora, the war minister, and the officers of the regular Piedmont army refused to recognize Garibaldi as a military leader and forced Cavour to put the *Cacciatori delle Alpi* directly under his ministry.

The *Cacciatori* were formed into three brigades. The first was led by Enrico Cosenz, who had recently fought with Manin in the battle for Venice; the second was led by Giacomo Medici, the young officer who came with Garibaldi from South America; and the third was led by Nicolai Arduino, who had fought in the campaigns of 1848 and 1849. Nino Bixio, an officer from the Roman campaign, was given the command of one of Arduino's battalions and Menotti Garibaldi (eighteen years old) was one of fifty scouts. Among the volunteers were the five Cairoli brothers from Milan—Benedetto, Ernesto, Enrico, Giovanni, and Luigi. Only Benedetto was to survive the wars. He later became Prime Minister of Italy.

On 16 May, the *Cacciatori* left Genoa by train for Biella, crossed the Ticino on 21 May, and arrived in Varese on 23 May.

Word soon came that the Austrian Lieutenant Marshall Urban was marching forward to Varese with six thousand infantry, two hundred cavalry, and eight cannons. Garibaldi immediately ordered the defense of the city by fortifying positions and building barricades. Three enemy rockets streaked across the night skies at 2:00 A.M. on 26 May and the battle was on. The Austrians tried to seize the south of the city, but were repulsed by forces led by Suzini and Sacchi. Regrouping and returning with more firepower, the Austrians attacked once again, only to be caught in a cross fire between newly positioned forces of Medici and Cozenz. Seizing the moment, Garibaldi charged out of the city with four companies and made a wheeling movement around the enemy's left flank and succeeded in penetrating their lines. The enemy was in flight and, by noon, Urban and his forces withdrew, leaving Varese in the hands of the victorious *Cacciatori*.

After a night of victorious back slapping, the morning found them anxious to search and destroy the enemy. Garibaldi decided that their next target would be Como, which was defended by a military installation at San Fermo. On the afternoon of 27 May, as Captain De Cristoforis's company made a suicidal frontal charge into the entrance of San Fermo, Garibaldi led the bulk of his forces up and over the hillsides to reach the unprotected rear of the city. The Austrians were surprised and, after heavy house to house fighting, were routed out of city. With the full force in pursuit, Garibaldi drove the Austrians all the way back to and out of Como. Garibaldi marched into Como at 9:00 P.M. that evening, victorious once again.

On the night of 30 May, Garibaldi attempted to protect his rear by an assault on the Austrian force at Laveno on Lake Maggiore. A detachment was sent to outflank the town while a frontal attack stormed the gates under Captain Landi. The results were disastrous as the flanking force got lost and Landi's men were beaten back with severe casualties. Garibaldi was furious and berated the wounded Landi unmercifully. It was such a disappointment after the successes at Varese and Como.

Meanwhile, Urban, with a force of fourteen thousand, marched on to Varese and overtook it on 31 May.

Garibaldi realized his precarious situation but, unknown to him, Victor Emmanuel and his army had defeated the Austrians at Palestro and were marching east. A few days later, a Piedmont-Franco army defeated the Austrians at Novara and had crossed the Ticino River on their way to Varese. Once this was known to him, Garibaldi was relatively safe to move freely and decided to hound Lieutenant Marshal Urban, who now was in full retreat. The *Cacciatori delle Alpi* took Lecco on 6 June and arrived at Bergamo on 8 June only to find the Austrians had already left.

All the time, since the start of the campaign, Garibaldi's forces were swelling dramatically; volunteers were coming from every walk of life and from all corners of the peninsula. Conservative estimates put the count at ten thousand strong; a considerable number more than Cavour had envisaged. Discipline became a problem; robberies and looting were commonplace. Cavour and the Piedmont general staff were concerned over the increasing power of Garibaldi.

After the *Cacciatori* entered Brescia on 13 June, he received orders to attack Tre Ponti, a fortress held by 200,000 Austrians. Garibaldi was incensed by the senseless orders that would put his men at jeopardy and exclaimed, "They wanted to make fools of us, but they have gone to tragic extremes." The Piedmontese generals did not want the 1859 campaign to be a series of victories for Garibaldi and feared his postwar popularity.

Unable to countermand an order, Garibaldi ordered his men to attack Tre Ponti on 15 June, despite the outrageous odds against them. They took a severe beating and lost many courageous men. Only the wily maneuvers of Garibaldi prevented total annihilation. Elated by his first victory, Urban didn't press his advantage and allowed the *Cacciatori* to retreat to Salo. From there, they were ordered to guard the Alpine pass of Passo dello Stelvio, far from the hostilities. Nothing of note happened for the rest of the war and all news was of the Franco-Piedmontese victories.

Two horrific battles (24 June) at San Martino (Piedmontese)

and Solferino (French) were won by the Franco-Piedmontese forces at a tremendous cost to both sides (22,000 Austrian and 17,000 Franco-Piedmontese dead). Afterwards, Napoleon III demanded an armistice from Austria, which was converted later into a permanent peace at Villafranca on 11 July. Louis-Napoleon's motives on suing for an early peace were military and political. It would have been an enormous task to dislodge the remaining Austrian forces from Lombardy. England, although in favor of the Italian cause, did not like the expansion of the French Empire on the continent. Prussia could not be expected to stay out of the war for long and would side with Austria. Also, the Catholics in France were opposed to the loss of temporal power of the Pope if Austria was completely driven out of Italy.

Under a secret agreement between Cavour and Napoleon III, prior to the outbreak of the war, Lombardy was to be annexed by Piedmont. In return for her help, France was to receive the city of Nice and the province of Savoy. In addition, the Central Italian States were to be united under a single monarchy controlled by the French.

Garibaldi was furious over the surrender of Nice, his birthplace, to that "fox of a Bonaparte." He delivered an impassioned speech to the Piedmont parliament, but received little satisfaction. He, with his forces, marched to Florence at the request of a military alliance in central Italy that was determined to rebuff the control of the French monarchy. This greatly disturbed Cavour and he feared Garibaldi would be an integral part in upsetting the precarious political balance he had gained. Cavour implored the king to demand Garibaldi's resignation. (Victor Emmanuel was the only Piedmontese the general would listen to at this moment in time.) Garibaldi obeyed his king and resigned on 16 November 1859, but publicly chastised particular political elements who generated "the fox-like policy that for the moment is holding up the triumphant progress of the Italian movement."

Italian diplomats were more than pleased with the outcome of the Second War of Independence, but Garibaldi and his supporters (*Garibaldini*) were less than pleased. Plotting and scheming, waiting for the opportune moment, they began making plans for a daring expedition which, when it came, was to be the most miraculous in Italian history.

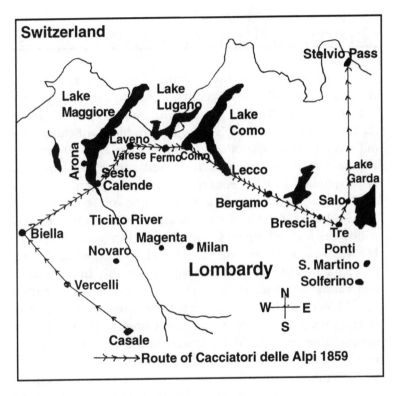

Garibaldi's Alpine Campaign 1859

Chapter XIII: Amorous Adventures

An interesting interlude from Garibaldi's military accomplishments has to be taken here to delve into the private life of the man. On his return from America, he gained a reputation as quite a lady's man. Due to his glorification as a military and romantic hero, Garibaldi was besieged by amorous advances from well-to-do, sophisticated, and cultured women. He responded with the energy of an insatiable lothario, which only embellished his persona as a romantic celebrity.

Garibaldi did not have the appearance of an overpoweringly handsome Italian figure, as described in most romance novels. He was five feet seven inches tall and bowlegged, had curly reddish hair and was light complected—hardly the tall, dark, and handsome type. Short in size but sturdy in build with a barrel-like chest, he bestowed an ominous presence if you chose to cross his path. Gifted with fast reactions, Garibaldi was an excellent swordsman. Many artisans of the period painted his image leading men with an unsheathed saber mounted upon a white stallion. It had to be a dramatic moment to have seen this and heard his order to charge—"*Avanti*"—all before movies and television were invented. He did possess a majestic face, a stone-like forehead and a unique profile with brown eyes that "penetrated your inner soul." Many women remarked about those eyes, eyes that revealed one's most intimate secrets, that seemed to undress on the spot. Undeniably, he possessed enormous energy on the battlefield; it can be assumed his wiry constitution enamored him to all in the boudoir. His dalliances reverberated throughout Europe.

In fact, he had become engaged to a widow upon his 1854 visit to London. Mrs. Emma Roberts was a rich and intelligent woman who became extremely fond of Garibaldi in a motherly way. Cultured and debonair, she was enthralled with this rugged celebrity and took pleasure in training him in the ways of the sophisticated. Three hour dinners with servants that reacted to your every move was not a lifestyle with which the general was comfortable. However, in his lonely state, he proposed marriage and she accepted; neither of them anticipating an early ceremony. When he returned to his family in Nice, she followed him with her friend, Jesse White, who also was enamored with Garibaldi. Jesse White was the daughter of an English shipbuilder and had a free spirit; she was the prototype of a modern day feminist. She was clever, adventurous, and never shied from any undertaking or experience. When the general developed his home at Caprera in the fall of 1855, the engagement to Mrs. Roberts lost its priority and the two women returned to London. Garibaldi would renew this romantic triangle on a subsequent visit to England as well as remain friends with the two women for life.

Garibaldi had brought a maidservant to Caprera to tend to the household duties as well as be a nanny to his children. Battistina Ravello was the poor, unschooled, and ignorant daughter of a seaman from Nice. She was unattractive, if not downright ugly, with crude mannerisms, but she seemed to arouse Garibaldi's prurient interest and became his mistress. In time (1859), she bore him a daughter named Anita who grew up to be a wild, untamed, rakish creature not unlike her mother.

At Caprera in 1857, he was visited by a German novelist by the name of Marie Esperance, Baroness von Schwartz, who wanted to translate Garibaldi's memoirs into German. She was a twice married divorcee (her first husband had committed suicide) and the twenty-six-year-old daughter of a Hamburg banker. Traveling alone, she was an educated, cosmopolitan, clever, aggressive, and opinionated woman as well as physically desirable. At age fifty, the general was swept away with ardor for the young sophisticate. After many meetings at Caprera and at La Maddalena, the two became romantically involved under the very jealous eye of Battistina, his servant. In fact, with

Battistina not more than fifty yards away, Garibaldi proposed marriage and, to his dismay, was rejected. The baroness had no desire to live among the hardships at Caprera under the accusing eye of Battistina. She was accustomed to the finest comforts of the continent. The general was crushed by her refusal, but did not let the reversal diminish his fervor for Mme. Schwartz and they remained an item for years. After the cessation of hostilities in 1859, she accompanied him to Bologna only to find out that Battistina had given birth to Garibaldi's child. That news and Garibaldi's sudden lack of interest had Mme. Schwartz leaving for other parts of Europe. She did publish his memoirs in 1861 under the alias of Elpis Melena.

The truth of the matter (losing his intensity for Mme. Schwartz) was that Garibaldi was in love with someone else. Marchesina Giuseppina Raimondi was the illegitimate daughter of a collaborator, Marquis Raimondi, who had an impressive estate at Fino. Garibaldi had met this seventeen-year-old at Como as a courier; she delivered messages through the Austrian lines. After the war in 1859, Garibaldi visited the family's villa at Fino to renew his friendship with the marquis and pursue his fondness for the adorable Giuseppina, who had turned eighteen. After many visits to the family's home at Fino, he professed his love and asked her to marry him. At fifty- two years of age, he implored upon her, "I am in no state to be able to wait . . . Yours for life—whatever may be."

The wedding was set for Wednesday, 24 January 1860, with all the ceremonial rites of the church. His daughter Teresa (she preferred Teresa, now, to Teresita), just turning fifteen, was a bridesmaid and many friends were in attendance, although few approved of the marriage. The marriage ceremony was short but dignified and Garibaldi, walking out of the chapel with his new bride, seemed most proud and serene. He was at the doorway receiving the congratulations and good tidings of guests when a man approached and handed him a letter.

It was a condemning revelation on Giuseppina's amorous romp the previous evening. She had been with a lover the night before they took their vows. Garibaldi was dumbfounded as he read the letter and, ignoring other well-wishers, took Giuseppina aside and asked with uncharacteristic rancor, "Is it true?" She looked at the letter and sheepishly admitted that it was. "Then," he shouted, "you are *una puttana*, a whore!" What happened next is disputed by historians; many explanations have been given, but none agreed on all aspects of the moment. What was sure was that Garibaldi was furious. He thought he was made the fool. Grim faced and silent, he mounted his white charger and slowly trotted away from the chapel into the sunset. Garibaldi would never see the Marchesina again although she unsuccessfully tried to visit him at Caprera in 1861. She never married again until Garibaldi received an annulment in 1880. She died in 1919.

Garibaldi renewed his relationship with Mme. Schwartz soon after this romantic disappointment. With Teresa and Signora Deideri, they visited the ashes of his beloved Anita at the Guiccoli farm at Mandriole. With the subsequent interruption and separation caused by other military adventures, Mme. Schwartz departed again but remained a good friend to the general, assisting him in gaining some military intelligence for some of his campaigns. With his heroic star just ascending in 1860, it is taken for granted that his amorous adventures continued in succeeding years.

Garibaldi was pressured to obtain an annulment of his marriage to the Marchesina to legitimatize his children of later years. It seems that the general had three more children by a servant woman who was brought to Caprera in 1866 to nursemaid the children of his daughter, Teresa. Francesca Armosino, strong and course in her features, as was Battistina, gave him two daughters and a son. Clelia was born in 1867, Rosita in 1869 (she died in 1871), and Manlio in 1873. After a lengthy battle to obtain the annulment, Garibaldi married her in January 1880. He was seventy-three years old at the time.

CHAPTER XIV: THE THOUSAND

Following his resignation from the Piedmont Army in the fall of 1859, Garibaldi felt free to enter into any independent enterprise that perpetuated the ideal of a unified Italy. He had been secretly conspiring with influential patriots to embark on a southern military expedition; there had been a strong feeling for some time that Sicily and Naples were ripe for liberation. Ferdinand II, King of the Bourbon States, had recently died and political unrest was universal. Francis II, his son and heir to the throne, was twenty-three and inept at handling the monarchy. In fact, the populace was rebellious in response to the tyrannical machinations of the new king. Time was right for some leadership to usurp this rebellious fervor and use it to drive the foreigners from Italy. Garibaldi was destined to be that leader.

This was not to be an easy task. Support, funds, guns, etc. had to be acquired. Garibaldi had consistently denied this endeavor for two reasons; he didn't believe the Sicilians had the resolve for a long bloody campaign and King Emmanuel had asked him not to pursue such a wild undertaking. Despite this, Garibaldi sent coconspirators to Sicily (Mme. Schwartz traveled to the island as a tourist) to ascertain the mood of the people for revolution. Knowing that their success was linked to Garibaldi's leadership, Sicilian patriots rebelled in open insurrection on 4 April 1860 to prove the resoluteness of their purpose. Uprisings broke out in Palermo, Messina, and Catania under the supervision of Rosolino Pilo and Francesco Riso. The effort was woefully inadequate and the surviving liberators fled to the mountains for refuge. (Riso was killed in Palermo.) However, the report sent back to the general did not reflect the gravity of the results and implored upon him to come to their aid. After a long discussion with his advisors, Garibaldi acquiesced and agreed to lead an armed expedition to Sicily.

Francesco Crispi was sent to Milan to procure arms and raise money for the "Million Rifles Fund." (Crispi was later to become Premier of Italy.) Bixio returned to Genoa to consult with the *Garibaldini* General Staff and to acquire ships to transport the expedition south. Garibaldi, in an attempt to gain support, made a request to the king that the Reggio Brigade be placed at his disposal. Victor Emmanuel consulted with Cavour and both agreed that it would be perilous in the eyes of the European community to assign a Piedmont unit to an avowed revolutionary. Cavour was more adamant about his refusal after receiving a wire from the Piedmont consul in Sicily that proclaimed the rebellion of 4 April a total failure.

Garibaldi and his followers stubbornly refused to give up their plan for an incursion somewhere in Italy, if not into Sicily. On 12 April, Medici, Bixio, Bertani, and Finzi began recruiting troops and the word was spread up and down the peninsula for patriots. On 15 April, Garibaldi moved his headquarters into a suburb of Genoa called Quarto, but he was not completely convinced of the merit of a Sicilian adventure. There were many a tumultuous discussions by the General Staff at the Villa Spinola, a small cottage in Quarto. Sacchi and Trecchi were against the expedition. Bixio, Crispi, Medici and Türr were in favor of it. Garibaldi vacillated between the two positions, unable to make up his own mind, his courage was even questioned. Despite all these doubts, worries, quarrels, and much soul searching, it was decided to go ahead with the preparations for the military expedition.

The American colonel, Samuel Colt, had sent a hundred of his famous pistols and, through devious means, a thousand rifles had arrived. Negotiations for ships were about to be finalized but, at the time of settlement, money was short. Giovan Fauche, a director of a Genoan steamship company, offered two ships at no cost if Garibaldi's forces would steal them. Fauche was later dismissed from his position and joined the *Garibaldini* in Sicily.

Time was now a factor. Cavour was besieged by the European powers to stop this expedition as its formation was rumored all over the continent. It was decided to sail on 6 May before the government had time to intercede. On the night of 5 May, Bixio and thirty men commandeered two ships in Genoa harbor and moved them south. Their was no resistance, as the ships were prepared ahead of time for boarding. The volunteers of the expedition assembled on the beach at Quarto were transferred to the *Piemonte* and the *Lombardo* by small fishing boats. Around midnight, Garibaldi descended to the beach, dressed in his classic red shirt and poncho, to oversee the embarkation of the 1,089 men. The total expeditionary force was 1,217 including those on the ships and other volunteers who were to come aboard at Piombino. Garibaldi took command of the *Piemonte*, which followed the slower *Lombardo* commanded by Bixio. The two ships left the Ligurian shores of Quatro as dawn broke on 6 May 1860.

Shortly after departure, it was learned that the ammunition was left on shore. It was too late to turn back and a decision was made to stop at Talamone on the Tuscan coast to acquire supplies. When they arrived, Türr went to the local garrison at Orbetello with a letter from Garibaldi which claimed the invasion had full support of the king. The ammunition was loaded aboard the ships before the commander of the garrison could check the verification of the request. Before they sailed, a proclamation written by Garibaldi was read to men of both ships:

"The mission of this corps will be, as it always has been, based on complete sacrifice for the regeneration of the fatherland. The brave *Cacciatori delle Alpi* have served and will serve their country with the devotion and discipline of the best kind of soldiers, without any other claim than the satisfaction of their consciences. Not rank, not honor, not reward have enticed these brave men. They returned to the seclusion of private life when danger disappeared. But now that the hour of battle has come again, Italy sees them once more in the foremost rank, joyful, willing, ready to shed their blood for her. The war-cry of the *Cacciatori delle Alpi* is the same as that which reechoed from the banks of the Ticino twelve months ago

Italia e Vittorio Emanuele,

and this war-cry, from your lips, will strike terror into the enemies of Italy."

A few of the Republicans aboard took exception to the mention of the monarchy and deserted the force and their place in history. The "Thousand," as they were later to be known, set sail again on 9 May after leaving 130 volunteers at Talamone under Zambianchi, as a diversionary force, to invade the Papal States.

The two day voyage was uneventful except that the men became acquainted with one another and became a cohesive fighting unit. They were from all corners of Italy and Europe. Fifty percent of the volunteers were students, followed by business men, landowners, doctors, lawyers, clerks, shopkeepers, and engineers. The average age was twenty, the youngest was eleven (Giuseppe Marchetti), and five men were in their sixties. The Thousand also included four Hungarians, three Austrians, three Swiss, three Frenchmen, one Englishman, and one Greek; the rest were Italian, including the five Cairoli brothers. There were a few musicians aboard who continually sang a song in honor of this historic moment. It was called "Garibaldi's Hymn" and was sung on the battlefields and continued to be heard many years after hostilities had subsided. Also, the colors red, white, and green with the arms of the House of Savoy, introduced into battle in 1848 by Charles Albert, were proudly displayed as the national flag.

On the morning of 11 May 1860, the port of Marsala on the western coast of Sicily appeared on the horizon. The Thousand and Garibaldi were feverish in their passion to begin this momentous invasion. All of Europe focused on this small expeditionary force, which could possibly change Italy's status in the world.

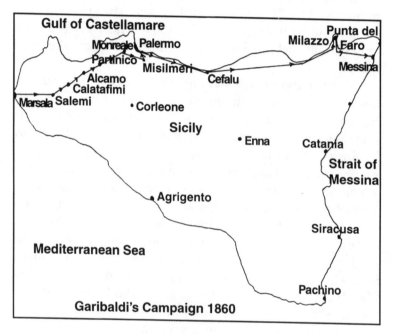

Sicily 1860

CHAPTER XV: INVASION OF SICILY

As the *Lombardo* and the *Piemonte* approached Marsala, two cruisers were seen docked in the harbor. Not anxious to confront a warship, Garibaldi was hesitant to proceed until confirmation was made that the ships were British. They hurriedly steamed for the harbor when a Neapolitan warship, the *Stromboli*, was spotted closing in from the south at great speed. The *Piemonte* got into the harbor safely and Garibaldi and his men disembarked quickly and headed for shore. The men of the *Lombardo* grounded at the entrance and hastily emptied into shore boats with stores and ammunition as the Neapolitan steamer approached. They all reached shore as the *Stromboli* opened fire on the Thousand with little success. They were out of range. However, the Neapolitans scuttled the *Lombardo* and apprehended the *Piemonte*, taking it out of the harbor. By this time, the *Garibaldini* were safely inside the gates of Marsala without any resistance. They only experienced one slight casualty from the landing. Garibaldi immediately sent messages to neighboring villages informing them of their success and pleading for their revolutionary support. Türr was responsible for destroying all forms of communication and cutting telegraph lines. Crispi, Garibaldi's political secretary, had quickly gotten the ruling class of Marsala to agree to a document that proclaimed the Bourbons had ceased to rule in Sicily and designated Garibaldi to assume the dictatorship in the name of Victor Emmanuel.

On the next morning, the *Garibaldini* marched out of Marsala across the flat desert and into the cultivated prairie of the interior. Horses were procured for Garibaldi and a few officers, but the rest of the Thousand were on foot on a hot sunny day. That evening they rested at the medieval tower of Rampagallo in the open field although the general slept in a tent. That night they were joined by peasant volunteers who were untrained and poorly armed, some with just picks and pitchforks as weapons. These bans of "little fellows" or *picciotti*, as they were known, were to grow in numbers with each town Garibaldi entered.

The next morning (13 May), they marched to the mountainous sanctuary of Salemi without incident. The panorama was breathtaking. In fact, as they followed the narrow path up to this town, with its medieval streets and buildings, the bell towers rang out and the populace welcomed the Thousand, shouting praises for Victor Emmanuel and Garibaldi. A thousand *picciotti* joined the ranks of the *Garibaldini* and more were rumored to be on the way. The dictatorship, in turn, announced that Bourbon taxes were abolished to the ecstatic satisfaction of the Sicilians.

Twenty-five thousand Neapolitan troops existed on Sicilian soil in 1860 with the main force centralized in and around Palermo. Upon notice of Garibaldi's landing, General Landi was dispatched from Palermo with a force of three thousand, including artillery to Alcamo, high above the gulf of Castellamare. Eventually, the Neapolitans advanced to Calatafimi, a town at the junction of the roads from Salemi and Trapani with those to Alcamo and down to Palermo. General Landi was seventy years old, frail, and not an aggressive commander. His indecisiveness allowed Garibaldi to consolidate his position, gaining volunteers, ammunition, and one cannon. The general also had ordered La Masa to infiltrate the interior of the island and rally the populace to their cause.

On the morning of 15 May, the forces of Garibaldi marched (eight miles) to the summit of Pietralunga, overlooking Calatafimi, and dug in. For hours, in eerie silence, the two forces stared at each other across the valley that separated them. Garibaldi, perched on high ground, observed the movement of the Neapolitan troops on Pianto di Romano (the hill opposite Pietralunga) and calmly lit a cigar. He liked his defensive position and did not care to attack such a superior force.

Finally, at noon, the Neapolitan bugles blared across the valley as if to signal the start of a duel. Garibaldi responded by having his bugler sound the reveille of Como. The battle was on! The Neapolitans started by descending into the valley and charging up the slope of the Pietralunga, firing as they came. The *Garibaldini* countercharged and turned the enemy back into the valley and up the slope of Pianto di Romano. The slope of Pianto di Romano was terraced with walled gardens and proved to be a formidable arena, fighting for a terrace at a time at close range. Garibaldi was seen in the middle of the battle, his talented saber in hand. The progress was slow—terrace by terrace—and costly. The *Garibaldini* gradually slowed to a stop and were held down for hours without any gain. At 3:00 P.M., Bixio came to the general, who had taken cover on one of the last terraces and was advised to withdraw. Garibaldi sprung to his feet with saber raised, as if something had stung him, and shouted, "Here we make Italy or die." He led and inspired his men to conquer the last few yards of contested ground, driving the enemy down the other side of the hill and back to Calatafimi in full retreat. The battle was over by 5:00 P.M.

The *Garibaldini* sank to the earth on the Pianto di Romano, victorious but too exhausted to pursue the routed forces. The Garibaldini suffered 210 casualties (thirty dead and 180 wounded). One of those wounded was Menotti Garibaldi, shot in the hand. The wounded were taken to Vita in the small peasant carts that are so colorful in Sicily.

The Neapolitans were astounded by the suicidal charges of the *Garibaldini*, which filled the ranks with bewilderment. Frenzied troops that had no regard for their well-being led by an invincible, fanatical leader created an image that was both fear-inspiring and terrifying. Landi, knowing his remaining troops were not psychologically prepared to test the *Garibaldini* again, left Calatafimi for Palermo via Alcamo and Partinico after midnight on 16 May.

The battle had reinforced the Sicilians' mystical aura of Giuseppe Garibaldi. Fires were lit on every hillside surrounding

Palermo, which spread the news of the success of the insurrection and the coming of their liberator. Local revolts and vicious attacks on the Bourbons were ubiquitous. In fact, in Partinico, as Landi's troops passed through, rebellion was so intense that it turned into an anarchistic orgy, so vicious that Garibaldi thought it to be excessive and repulsive.

Garibaldi ordered Pilo and La Masa with their forces to advance to the high ground above Palermo at Monreale. Monreale, four miles from Palermo upon Mount Caputo, was the home of the Monreale Cathedral built in the twelfth century by a Norman, William II. Garibaldi, with the remaining Thousand and three thousand Sicilian volunteers, marched on to Partinico and eventually to Renda, where the majestic city of Palermo came into view.

The city of Palermo was in a frenzy with rumors. The citizens were anxious about the ongoing events. Many had left the city for refuge, anticipating the worst. Shops were closed, many homes were boarded up, and every day commerce was minimal. Foreign ships had entered the harbor to protect their consulates. The Bourbons had twenty-one thousand Neapolitan soldiers, ample artillery, several warships, and a impregnable fortress in Palermo. Garibaldi realized a frontal attack on such a fortified position would be disastrous if not suicidal.

General Lanzi had arrived on 16 May from Naples to assume command of the Neapolitan forces and immediately sent three thousand additional troops to Monreale. These men were under the competent leadership of Colonel Von Michel and Major Bosco, the most courageous and combative officers of the Bourbon forces. On 21 May, they charged out of their positions at Monreale and aggressively attacked the revolutionary forces in the hills. It was a vicious skirmish with heavy losses on both sides and especially devastating to Pilo's forces. (Pilo was killed.) Garibaldi's position now became precarious, only miles from the action. A brilliant maneuver evolved that was named later by military historians as "the diversion of Corleone."

Garibaldi decided to detour his approach to Palermo by other roads via Corleone, Parco, and Piana Greci. At dusk, Orsini led the revolutionary forces south up the mountain toward Corleone. Dragging a disabled cannon, brush, and large banners, they created as much dust as possible. Noticed by the Bourbons as a movement by a large force retreating to the hills, Von Michel and Bosco took off in hot pursuit. Three miles into the march, Garibaldi and the major force of *Garibaldini* turned off on a little known path circling to the east and doubled back toward Palermo. The Neapolitans continued to pursue Orsini's small force and the dusty illusion of a larger force toward Corleone. On the morning of 22 May, the *Garibaldini* staggered into Parco at the very outskirts of Palermo. By this maneuver, Garibaldi gained at least two days distance from Von Michel.

Garibaldi immediately sent orders to La Masa to come down from the hills at Gibilrossa to defend the east flank. On 24 May, Garibaldi became aware that the remaining forces at Monreale had come out to search and destroy his position. To avoid a frontal attack, the revolutionary forces retreated to Piana Greci. The Monreale forces despaired in finding the main force of the *Garibaldini* and, after vicious attacks by local peasants, turned back to Palermo. Von Michel was slow in regrouping after he discovered the ruse set in motion by Garibaldi. He was furious about falling for such a trick. On 25 May, Garibaldi ordered a march east to Misilmeri and joined the forces of La Masa. All was in readiness for the attack and liberation of Palermo.

CHAPTER XVI: PALERMO

At 3:00 A.M. on Sunday, 26 May, La Masa descended from the surrounding hills with three thousand *picciotti*, a poorly disciplined force made up of Sicilian peasants armed with pitchforks, blunderbusses, and *lupari* (the traditional shotgun of the island). The Thousand now numbered 750 due to sickness and casualties. Together, with the *picciotti*, they hardly represented a formidable adversary to the sixteen thousand Neapolitan troops with superior artillery present in Palermo. This did not count the two battalions with Von Michel chasing Orsini's dust to Corleone.

A revolutionary war council convened and deliberation began as what to do next, *a plan de guerre*. Garibaldi surrounded himself with many of his faithful as well as some newcomers, military men who had impressive records. La Masa, Bixio, and Menotti Garibaldi were in attendance. In addition, Colonels Türr, Talecki, and Tüköry were present. A new member of the war council was Ferdinand Eber, a Hungarian who, as a journalist in Palermo, had firsthand knowledge of fortifications in and around Palermo. The town of Parco, just outside of Palermo at the foot of the mountains, was heavily garrisoned, thousands of enemy troops lined the roads leading into Palermo from Monreale and Porazzi, and the western and northern limits of Palermo had pockets of Neapolitan militia. Eber stated that if the revolutionary forces could somehow get into the center of the city, they would find it relatively undefended and the local partisans would rally to their aid. The optimum access to Palermo, Eber continued, would be by way of the Porta Termini, which was lightly defended. This gate was the southeast entrance to Palermo, a few miles from Garibaldi's encampment.

The Neapolitans were looking for a Garibaldi attack from the west. At six in the morning, the decision was made to move on to Palermo via *Porta Termini* with utmost haste. Garibaldi said, "Tomorrow, I shall enter Palermo as victor, or the world will never see me again among the living."

That evening, the revolutionary forces descended upon the *Conca D'Oro*—the beautiful hillside of orange groves and olive trees that leads down to Palermo. At the head of the column was Missori with a small force of thirty veterans followed by La Masa and the Sicilians (*picciotti*). Next came Garibaldi with two battalions, led, respectively, by Bixio and Carini and the Genoese *carbineri* between the two. It was agreed by all that silence was essential to create the element of surprise.

However, as the passionate Sicilians reached the *Ponte dell' Ammiraglio* and saw the lights of Palermo, they shot wildly into the air, shouting, "Palermo! Palermo!" The surprise attack that Garibaldi envisioned had vanished. The militia defending the bridge into the city awoke and began returning fire. The Sicilians panicked and ran back into the orange groves. Garibaldi came onto the scene exhorting the *picciotti* to advance, but to no avail. He then ordered Tüköry and Bixio's battalion to attack the bridge and could be heard shouting the infamous order, "*Avanti! Avanti!*" ("Forward! Forward!") Tüköry, with a small force, threw themselves at the *Ponte dell' Ammiraglio*, but were repelled by intense rifle fire. Tüköry was wounded. (He was to die a few days later of gangrene.) This only set the *picciotti* into further panic, falling over each other, scrambling for safe ground.

Again, Garibaldi came on the scene yelling, "*Avanti, Cacciatori! Avanti! Entrate nel centro!*" ("Forward! Into the heart of the town!") Two companies of Bixio's battalion and the Genoese Carbineers were stirred to charge the bridge. In less than an hour, the bridge was taken and the next bridge, *Ponte delle Teste*, was easily overcome. The Thousand now were in a rush to enter the city via the *Porta Termini*. Bixio, who was injured but extracted the bullet himself, was one of the first to enter Palermo. Garibaldi remained behind to drive the *picciotti* out of the gardens, where they had taken refuge, and coerce them to move forward toward the city.

As the *Garibaldini* entered the city amid few cheers from the residents, they moved cautiously to the *Fiera Vecchi* (Ancient Market) with little resistance. At first, the multitude of Palermitans did not show themselves, refusing to join the liberators. The unlimited support from the townspeople that Eber prophesied was not happening. Centuries of invasions and mistrust of foreign invaders were deeply ingrained in the Sicilian psyche and still are to this day. Finally, the *picciotti* regrouped from the orange groves and vineyards and entered the city, exhorting their fellow citizens to come out and support the revolution. Hearing the Sicilian dialect shouted from the streets, the Palermitans slowly assured themselves that this was not an invasion by outsiders but by their own people. One by one, and then by tens and hundreds, they descended upon the streets in recognition that this was their ultimate emancipation. The populace had finally joined the fight.

All of Palermo was jubilant over the liberation of their city. Every bell tower was ringing with excitement. Just at the peak of this exhilaration, bombardment started to pummel the city from the Neapolitan ships in the harbor, from the batteries at the fortress at Castellamare, and from the Royal Palace. It was devastating. The congested center of the city was decimated by the constant barrage. Entire neighborhoods were destroyed, families lost forever and fires were raging throughout Palermo. In three days, three hundred Palermitans were killed and five hundred wounded; bodies were strewn over the streets of Palermo and, in time, the stench of death was everywhere. Garibaldi moved on to *Quattro Cantoni* at the center of the city and established the headquarters of the *Garibaldini*.

During those three days, military skirmishes were ubiquitous and neither side could sustain an advantage. The Sicilians did succeed in clearing the streets, but were still surrounded by the Neapolitan forces and their incessant cannons. When Garibaldi was told that a Neapolitan detachment had come out from the cathedral, he led fifty of his most seasoned veterans and Sicilian rebels to repel the force. When the enemy saw this small unit marching toward them under the leadership of Garibaldi, fear gripped their hearts and they rushed back to their refuge. The invincible aura of the "great" Garibaldi was gaining gigantic proportions. The bombardment did not get the desired result, but only increased the resolve of the populace to side with the *Garibaldini*. Many of their churches and most prized religious artifacts were lost forever. This senseless destruction has never been forgotten by the Palermitans.

The commander of the Neapolitans (General Lanza) realized that with most of his forces holed up in the Royal Palace, he was cut off from the sanctuary of his ships in the harbor, as well as from the rest of his forces. He knew he could not last if this was to be the status quo, though Von Michel had returned from his wild-goose chase to Corleone. They were cut off from supplies of food and ammunition. Against the advice of his chiefs of staff, he suggested a truce and a conference through English Admiral Mundy, aboard the *HMS Hannibal* in the harbor. It was accepted immediately and all hostilities ceased on 30 May.

That afternoon (2:15 P.M.), Garibaldi, dressed in all the splendor of a Piedmontese general, and Francesco Crispi went aboard the *HMS Hannibal* to deliberate with General Letizia of the Neapolitan Army. The talks did not start well. General Letizia protested the attendance of the foreign ship captains present in Admiral Mundy's conference room. Also, he derided Garibaldi's title of dictator and refused to confer with him. The foreign powers responded with indignation—especially the French and American captains. Admiral Mundy was disturbed by the dictatorial tone of General Letizia and gave him an ultimatum, to either proceed with the conference under the auspices of the foreign powers or leave his ship and terminate all talks.

The general acquiesced and began to read the articles of agreement as submitted by his superior, General Lanza. Garibaldi passively accepted the first four articles, but when the fifth article was read: "That the municipality should address a humble petition to His Majesty, the king, laying before him the real wishes of the town, and that this petition should be submitted to His Majesty," Garibaldi rose to his feet in a rage. He exclaimed, "No! The time for humble petitions, either to the king or to any other person is past, besides there is no longer any municipality! I am the municipality! I refuse my assent!" Astonished by such a verbal outburst, General Letizia folded up the papers before him and, with increased sarcasm, said, "Then, sir, unless this article is agreed to, all communication between us must cease." Garibaldi responded with such rancor that it was obvious he had lost his composure; his face was red with rage, his eyes wild with fury. General Letizia retorted with equal enmity.

Before leaving the ship, General Letizia grudgingly agreed to a cease-fire until noon the next day. Garibaldi returned to the *Quattro Cantoni* and delivered an impassioned speech to the citizens and the *Garibaldini* to prepare them for the battle ahead. New barricades were feverishly built during the night and every possible weapon was brought out into the open; additional ammunition and artillery were acquired from sympathetic foreign sources. This so impressed General Lanza in the morning that he requested an additional three-day extension of the truce. After repeated extensions, Neapolitan indecision and the reluctance of the king to put such a large command at jeopardy forced the Neapolitans to capitulate on 6 June 1860. Under the signed agreement, the Neapolitans were to abandon the palace and other positions within the city except for the garrison at Castellamare. They were to march out in full military protocol and to assemble at the foot of Mount Pellegrino to await naval transportation to Naples. The next morning, twenty thousand Neapolitan troops withdrew from Palermo under the protective eye of Garibaldi; the enemy marched though the city to the port amid jeers of the joyous Palermitans. It took until 19 June for the sailing of the last remnant of the Neapolitan army to depart. As the Neapolitan ships disappeared over the horizon, the people of Palermo realized their liberation had become a reality.

CHAPTER XVII: FINAL CONQUEST OF SICILY

Garibaldi began the arduous task of governing his new conquest, a totally new responsibility for him. He wisely gave Crispi, his Minister of the Interior, a freehand with the details of government. Francesco Crispi had been born in Ribera, Sicily and studied law in Palermo. He knew the subtlety of his fellow islanders. Crispi was adept in dealing with political intrigue and those who desired to limit Garibaldi's successes. The citizens of Palermo recovered the bodies of the dead from the rubble. Damaged buildings were restored where possible and others were torn down. The red shirts of the *Garibaldini* were seen everywhere helping in the labor but primarily maintaining civil order, which was becoming a problem. It seems that the Sicilians were less interested in national unity and more interested in social reforms for the island. The excessive retributions by the citizens toward the aristocracy who had exploited them for centuries required severe disciplinary action. This brought the *Garibaldini* in direct confrontation with the wishes of the Sicilian peasants, a chink in the armor that widened into a gulf between the two different Italian sensibilities. Governing the Sicilians was to be a problem for Garibaldi throughout his dictatorship.

On 19 June, Giacomo Medici arrived at the Gulf of Castellamare with the "second expedition" of 3,500 well-equipped men from Genoa. He joined the general in his new headquarters at the Royal Palace where, with the rest of his officers, they celebrated their recent successes. Constant diplomatic pressures were exerted on Garibaldi to annex Sicily in the name of the Piedmont-Sardinian monarchy, Victor Emmanuel. Garibaldi resisted these attempts, fearing the monarchy would not pursue his dream of unifying all of Italy. He declared, "I came to fight for all of Italy, not of Sicily alone. If we do not free and unite the whole of Italy, we shall never achieve liberty in any single part of her." This was all to the chagrin of Count Cavour.

Reinforcements were streaming into Palermo from all over the Mediterranean and Europe. America sent volunteers as well as contributions—a hundred thousand dollars from New York City alone. The new forces were organized into many divisions and battalions, maintaining their ethnicity wherever possible.

Garibaldi was informed of a massive concentration of Neapolitan forces at Milazzo over a hundred miles to the east, an obvious hurdle to the Strait of Messina and Calabria. The fortress at Milazzo lay on a small peninsula on the northeast tip of Sicily, defended by 2,500 troops and eight cannons on a plain south of the city. Fourteen hundred additional men with forty cannons remained in Milazzo. Bixio's division was directed to the southern coast of the island and marched eastward, arousing the population to join the movement. Türr's division marched eastward across the interior with the same purpose of gaining support from the masses. They were to meet at Punta del Faro on the Strait of Messina. Garibaldi, in the meantime, marched eastward along the coast, stopping at each village and town amid the raves and adulation of the people. In fact, at Cefalù, the reception was so great in front of the cathedral built by Roger II in the twelfth century, fears grew for the safety of the general as thousands crowded the small piazza trying to get a glimpse of their "liberator." On 19 July, Garibaldi came on the scene at Milazzo, observing the plain in front of the town as well as the fortifications in its center.

On the morning of 20 July, a three-prong attack was put into operation, designed to disable the enemy and bring victory. A small force under the leadership of Nichola Fabrizi was also sent up the road to Messina to repel any Neapolitan reinforcements. A frontal attack via the main road was to supported by flanking attacks from the coast. Unfortunately, the left flank was beaten back until Cosenz assumed command and slowed the retreat. The right flank, however, had advanced and beat the Neapolitans back to the harbor, but not without severe casualties. Garibaldi was constantly heard in the heat of the battle exhorting his men to charge. *"Avanti! Avanti!"* As he led one charge, Garibaldi had lost his mount and sprung to his feet with saber in hand. He and his aide-de-camp, Missori found themselves surrounded by a dozen Neapolitan cavalrymen. The leader of the unit recognized the general and, standing up in his stirrups and sword extended, charged Garibaldi, until Missori shot the horse under him. As he fell, he desperately lashed out, only to receive a deft blow from Garibaldi's saber, which nearly severed the Neapolitan's head from his shoulders. Missori instinctively shot two other horsemen as the general swirled around menacingly toward the others. Frightened by the loss of their leader and comrades, the rest of the Neapolitans galloped toward the bridge that led to town.

After a brief respite, Garibaldi had turned to the coast to check the progress of Cosenz when he observed a steamer offshore. It was the ten gun *Tüköry*, formerly the Neapolitan *Veloce*, whose crew had deserted the Bourbon service and had come to the assistance of the revolution. With the aid of a little skiff, Garibaldi embarked and directed the captain to take the ship closer to shore and bombard the troops that were impeding Cosenz's advance. As a result, the Neapolitans retreated into Milazzo and to the castle fortress, allowing the three-prong attack of the *Garibaldini* to complete its encirclement of Milazzo.

After three days of siege, the Royalist commander in the castle fortress at Milazzo, Colonel Bosco, was notified of Garibaldi's terms of an unconditional surrender. Bosco vehemently refused but semaphored to Messina for assistance. General Clary, the commander at Messina, was hesitant to release any of his fifteen thousand men when it was learned that a column of *Garibaldini* (Bixio and Türr) and thousands of partisans were marching north from Catania. After much indecision and contemplation, the war minister in Naples, with the assent of the king, agreed to rescue Bosco's forces and the allow capitulation of Milazzo to the dictator of Sicily.

On 23 July, four Neapolitan frigates appeared off the coast of Milazzo. General Anzani came ashore and directed all negotiations for surrender over the strenuous objections of Colonel Bosco. It was agreed that the Neapolitans would be allowed to leave the castle fortress, with all the livestock and material it contained turned over to Garibaldi. The Neapolitan troops (four thousand) embarked on the ships and returned to Naples on 24 July. Bosco went to Messina to resume the fight. However, on direction of the king and Naples, Messina opened its gates to Medici's troops on 28 July. On 1 August, Siracusa and Augusta fell and all of Sicily was in the hands of Garibaldi, except for a citadel in Messina.

Once again, Garibaldi was besieged with entreaties from Turin to halt his progress and by no means attempt a crossing to the mainland. Cavour was concerned with the recent successes of the *Garibaldini* and the possibility of a complete victory against Naples. He said, ". . . for if that happens a revolutionary system will take place of the monarchist party." Many rumors were flying in diplomatic circles and much duplicity was evident. An official letter from King Victor Emmanuel was directed through the usual channels and implored Garibaldi to cease and desist. A secret, second letter, sent without the knowledge of Count Cavour, contradicted the formal message of the first and advised the general as to how to respond. Garibaldi answered, "Your majesty knows the high esteem and love I bear you. But the present state of things does not allow me to obey you . . . If now, in face of all the calls that reach me, I delayed any longer I shall fail in my duty and imperil the sacred cause of Italy. Allow me then, Sire, this time to disobey you. As soon as I have fulfilled what I have undertaken, by freeing the peoples from a hated yoke, I will lay down my sword at your feet and obey you for the rest of my life."

France and Louis-Napoleon wanted to take action with an Anglo-France blockade, but were dissuaded by the English. Fearful of creating tensions between the two countries, Napoleon III was hesitant to interfere on his own. Consequently, Garibaldi was spared a confrontation with the major powers and could make preparations to cross the Strait of Messina. This was to be no easy task.

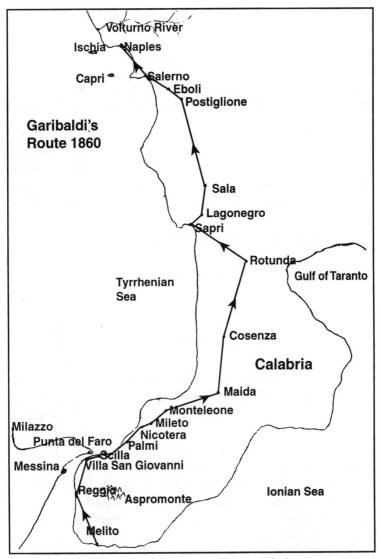

Garibaldi's Route to Naples 1860

CHAPTER XVIII: ADVANCE TO NAPLES

The battle of Milazzo was a great victory for Garibaldi but made at a great loss of men—eight hundred killed and wounded, casualties four times those suffered by the enemy. The effect of these losses was minimized by the thousands of volunteers that were streaming into Sicily to follow their glorified hero to higher levels of achievement. New reinforcements had arrived from Genoa, commanded by Colonel Pianciani, a force of six thousand men. The Thousand in Sicily had ballooned into twenty thousand veterans, volunteers, and peasants, but only one warship.

The Strait of Messina separates Sicily from the mainland and has historically been hazardous to crossings due to intense tidal currents. Villa San Giovanni and Altifiumara, on the mainland, lie directly across the strait from Punta del Faro (the narrowest width of the Strait of Messina at 1.6 miles) and could be seen to be well fortified. Two Neapolitan divisions defended Calabria with a force of seventeen thousand men and thirty-two cannons. In addition, no less then ten warships of the Neapolitan navy freely cruised the strait and presented an immense obstacle to any passage. Also, Count Cavour had ordered a warship under the captaincy of Admiral Persano to prevent any landing in Papal territory; the Piedmont army was on alert to guard the frontiers. The revolutionaries deemed that an attempt to invade the mainland was an exercise in futility. Some Sicilians lost their zest for battle and returned to their homes. The resilient Garibaldi went to the lighthouse at Punta del Faro daily to observe the enemy's fortifications and to ponder his next move. He refused to be sidetracked in his ultimate goal of a united Italy.

From Punta del Faro, a fleet of twelve small fishing boats and four hundred *Garibaldini* crossed the Strait of Messina on the starry night of 8 August. Unfortunately, they were spotted a few yards off the mainland and bombarded by the Neapolitan cannon. Only 150 men managed to make the shore and scurried to the hills of Aspromonte (a mountain range above the city of Reggio Calabria). They evaded the Bourbons sent out to apprehend them while building huge fires nightly to signal Garibaldi of their active resistance.

Garibaldi continued to show signs of embarkation at Punta del Faro by marching troops aimlessly about and amassing small boats—another ingenious ruse. Meanwhile, Bixio had acquired two steamers from the south side of the island and secretly brought them to Taormina, thirty miles south of Messina. On the night of 18 August, Garibaldi crammed 3,400 men aboard the *Franklin* and the *Torino* and set off for the southern coast of Calabria. The next morning, they successfully landed at Melito, south of Reggio, without incident and waited for their compatriots to join them from the hills.

Seventeen thousand Neapolitan troops were lodged in Lower Calabria but none south of Reggio, allowing the invasion force to freely move northward. By noon on 20 August, Garibaldi approached Reggio and was put upon by a large Royalist force commanded by Colonel Dusmet. A vicious battle ensued, and after a few hours, the enemy was repulsed and driven back to the Cathedral Square of the city. Losing little time, Garibaldi took to the offensive and routed the defending troops who fled for their lives. By evening, the Neapolitans surrendered when their leader, Colonel Dusmet, was shot and killed.

The capture of Reggio in such a short time was impressive and diplomatic quarters throughout the world were speechless with awe. Neapolitan casualties were small, but the volunteers had 147 wounded and killed. Bixio was wounded twice but refused to seek medical help until Garibaldi ordered him to bed with the sarcastic comment, "I suppose the balls that hit *you* are made of puff-paste." With this victory, the *Garibaldini* came into possession of two thousand rifles, thirty cannons, eight field pieces and, more importantly, the city of Reggio, which enabled more of the invasion force to cross the Strait of Messina.

On 22 August, Garibaldi marched north to the hills above Villa San Giovanni and hooked up with Cosenz and 1,300 reinforcements who had come across the strait when the Neapolitan navy had belatedly pursued the revolutionary landing at Melito. Garibaldi now commanded a force of five thousand men and was in the possession of valuable military material. The playing field was, indeed, getting more even. By a succession of additional landings behind the Neapolitan lines and the advance of Garibaldi's main force, the enemy found themselves often surrounded. Awed by the invincibility of Garibaldi and the Red-Shirts, the Neapolitan army had lost their desire to wage war and fled. Garibaldi fearlessly rode down among them in their flight and shouted, "Soldiers, you, as well as my companions, are the sons of Italy—remember that. You are at liberty. Whoever wishes to remain with us may apply to General Cosenz, your countryman, who has authority to enlist you. But whoever wishes may go home." By 24 August, all of Calabria was won with only the armed conflict at Reggio and smaller battles at Soluno and Villa San Giovanni. Large caches of ammunition, rifles, and cannons were confiscated on their march north to Scilla; reinforcements came in droves across the Strait of Messina. Revolts were ubiquitous in southern Italy, for the people were awaiting their savior—Giuseppe Garibaldi. The road to Naples lie open before him.

Meanwhile, major developments were mounting in Piedmont. Cavour was fearful that Garibaldi, with his new military successes, would remain headstrong and march on to Rome if Naples fell. France would never allow this to happen and the recent gains of the *Garibaldini* could possibly be lost. Cavour requested Napoleon III's permission to march south, through the Papal States, with the Piedmont army and the king, to intercept Garibaldi. Louis-Napoleon (Napoleon III), in political disfavor at home, did not want to put French troops at risk and assented to the proposal. Cavour and King Victor Emmanuel began their march south through the marshes with the intention of bypassing the Pope's province of Lazio.

The royalist king, Francis II, was busy amassing his troops outside Naples, along the river Volturno—a force of forty thousand men. Garibaldi continued his relentless march north through Mileto, Conzenza, Sapri and many other smaller villages and towns. After learning that the Neapolitan troops had abandoned Salerno, he entered with his entire general staff on 6 September amid wild jubilation and cheers—"*Viva! Viva Garibaldi!*" That same day, King Francis II left Naples aboard the *Messaggero*, taking refuge in the northern fortress at Gaeta. He would never see Naples again.

Soon after, Don Librio, the acting mayor of Naples, wrote to Garibaldi, "Naples awaits the Redeemer of Italy, that she might place her destiny in his hands." Garibaldi, aware of the Piedmont delegation marching south through the Papal States, was anxious to gain control of Naples. His officers wanted him to wait for the arrival of the rest of his forces, who were forty-eight hours away due to his rapid advance. They advised him to delay his entry at least twenty-four hours to allow the enemy forces to depart the city. Headstrong and determined, the general was not to be dissuaded and entered Naples on that very afternoon, 7 September, in an open carriage. Naples was enthralled at the presence of the great "liberator"; celebration and joy were everywhere. He went directly to the Royal Palace and, from a balcony, spoke to the throng. "You have a right to exult in this day. It is the beginning of a new epoch, not only for you but for the whole of Italy, of which Naples is the fairest part. It is, indeed, a day of glory and a holy day—a day which a people passes from the yoke of servitude to the rank of a free nation. I thank you for this welcome, not only for myself, but in the name of all Italy which will be made free and united with your help."

In due time, Garibaldi had thirty thousand troops at his disposal for the battle of Volturno, but only twenty thousand could be relied upon to fight a long, ongoing siege. The enemy was well dug in from Capua to Gaeta along the Volturno River, a distance of twelve miles, with the best of the Neapolitan army complemented by a large number of artillery. Garibaldi moved his headquarters to the Palace at Caserta and patrolled the hills with the aid of a telescope. He observed the movements of the Bourbon troops in the valley below and analyzed the fortifications thereof; he realized a full scale attack by his forces would be defeated by such a superior force. However, to wait could possibly allow Papal forces or even Austria to come to the aid of King Francis II. Also, the Piedmont army, with King Emmanuel, was marching south. Garibaldi deployed his forces along the Volturno in defensive positions and left for Sicily. His presence was needed in Sicily to settle some questions of ownership between land barons and the peasantry as well to quell the desire for immediate annexation.

In the general's absence, Türr took the initiative and crossed the Volturno to attack Caizzo and Capua. It proved disastrous, as the *Garibaldini* lost 135 men at Capua alone. As a further response, seven thousand Royalists moved against the force at Caizzo and drove them back across the river at a loss of 250 men to the revolutionaries. If the Neapolitans had continued their advance south with their superior numbers, they would have driven the leaderless *Garibaldini* from the valley and retaken Naples. However, the war ministers in Gaeta and the king were at dispute as what to do next. Their incertitude proved invaluable to Garibaldi and gave him the necessary time to regroup. Again, the *Garibaldini* were spared a fatal blow by the hesitation and indecisiveness of the enemy.

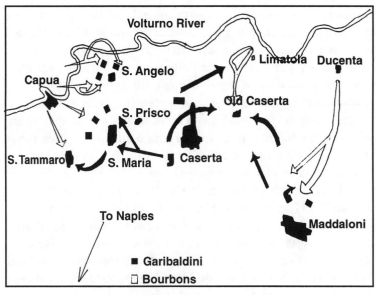

Battle of Volturno 1860

CHAPTER XIX: BATTLE OF VOLTURNO

Garibaldi returned to the Volturno on the afternoon of 19 September and was furious with the callous disregard for his defensive positions by Türr. In later memoirs, Garibaldi was negative in his opinion of Türr. ". . . supposed that no undertaking was beyond the powers of our bold volunteers." Only the hesitation of the Bourbon military hierarchy and the reappearance of the general prevented the Neapolitans from overrunning the *Garibaldini* and retaking Naples. In fact, there was a sizable lull in active military action until 1 October, other than small skirmishes. Garibaldi used this time to redeploy his forces, but only in a defensive posture.

Military analysts acclaim, "The Battle of Volturno" as the one and only time the *Garibaldini* fought a defensive battle. Frankly, the historians doubted Garibaldi's ability in a large battle. He was so effective in guerrilla warfare. The Royalist forces had at their disposal a force of fifty thousand men and forty-two cannons commanded by Marshal Ritucci. Garibaldi, on the other hand, defended a twelve-mile front with approximately twenty-five thousand troops and twenty cannons —a two-to-one disadvantage for the *Garibaldini*.

Sensing the imminent arrival of the Piedmont army, the Royalist forces attacked on 1 October. It was a multi-pronged attack at Sant' Angelo, Santa Maria, and San Tammaro, with King Francis II and his brothers appearing at the front to inspire confidence in the Neapolitan troops. In the early hours, the Royalists maintained pressure on Garibaldi's defensive positions and initially gained ground. However, countercharges by the *Garibaldini* soon eroded this advantage and the Volturno (the twelve-mile front) became embroiled in a massive struggle, the outcome of which was not clear. Garibaldi, in a sortie to Sant' Angelo, in a carriage with a few aides, was surrounded by the enemy. Captain Pratelli's Seventh Company came to his rescue, literally cutting a path for safety with bayonets.

Attacks and counterattacks continued along the Volturno for two days with the advantage tottering back and forth. The Neapolitans were extended around the outside of a semicircle that measured more than twelve miles, a strategy that effectively minimized their advantage of superior numbers. The revolutionary forces controlled the inner part of that semicircle and were not overextended. They could meet any new challenge swiftly from their condensed position with direct communications to the rear guard and Naples. It was still obvious that the Neapolitans could have attacked with their superior concentrated force at the middle of the resistance and been in a victorious march to Naples within twenty-four hours. Nevertheless, their military commanders had neither the capacity nor the resolve to do so. Casualties were high on both sides. The *Garibaldini* sustained 1,634 men killed or wounded, with an additional 389 missing or captured; the Neapolitans suffered 1,128 casualties, with 2,160 missing or as prisoners of war. The *Garibaldini* made up for their lesser numbers with military competence and a feverish desire to unite Italy. The Neapolitans, on the other hand, were anxious to surrender when the tide began to go against them. The Royalists did exactly that and capitulated on 2 October.

The importance of this battle was lost on some historians. If the Royalists had won The Battle of the Volturno, Garibaldi would have never seen a united Italy in his lifetime. Most definitely, Victor Emmanuel and his forces would not have advanced another kilometer in their southern march. The Neapolitans would have gained favor from the European powers, especially France. However, history proved otherwise and the Bourbon, Neapolitan, Kingdom of Two Sicilies was terminated. King Francis II took sanctuary with a rudimentary force in Gaeta and eventually fled to Rome and the protection of the Pope. The Spanish Bourbon dynasty had ruled Naples and Sicily since 1735. To the chagrin of the bourgeoisie, the ruling class owed the unity of modern Italy to a people's army. In 1860, the most powerful figure in Italy was Giuseppe Garibaldi.

With the exhilaration from their recent gains, supporters strongly urged Garibaldi to continue his march northward to Rome. Cavour was anxious as to what path he would follow and pleaded with the general's oldest friend, Augusto Vecchi, to correspond with Garibaldi, imploring him to give up his Roman designs. Vecchi wrote, ". . . Invite the king personally by a telegram to come quickly to Naples. And go to meet him. I ask this of you in the name of Italy, our mother, for whose greatness we two swore many years ago to make every kind of sacrifice."

Garibaldi had made up his mind long before receiving that correspondence. He realized a substantial force (all of the manpower he could muster) would be needed to lay siege to Rome. This would leave Naples, Calabria, and even Sicily vulnerable to the reorganizing efforts of the enemy. His volunteers would follow him anywhere, but to continue to Rome would be in total disobedience to the king, Cavour, and the Piedmont legislature; a civil war would result and Garibaldi could not allow that to happen. After many days of anguish and thought, he wrote to the king, "I congratulate your Majesty on the brilliant victories won by your brave General Cialdini and on their happy results . . . Since your Majesty is at Ancona, you must make the journey to Naples by land or sea. If I were informed in time, I would move forward my right wing to meet you, and would come in person to present my homage and to receive your orders as to the final operations."

Garibaldi met with Victor Emmanuel at Teano on the morning of 26 October 1860, and formally handed over the conquered territories (and the dictatorship of the Two Sicilies). The two exchanged pleasantries, but the king made it clear to Garibaldi that Piedmont monarchy would now take over the reins of all that the *Garibaldini* controlled. The king tried to ameliorate Garibaldi with rewards of titles, pension, and material possessions. Garibaldi would have none of it. Nonetheless, the general was adamant about the welfare of his men and the continuance of the war. To this request, deaf ears were turned to Garibaldi. In addition, Victor Emmanuel and, particularly Cavour, rescinded most of Garibaldi's reforms, laws, and appointments enacted during his dictatorship. In a shameless insult to Garibaldi and his men, the king failed to appear at a farewell parade for the *Garibaldini*. He had little regard for the "rabble" of the revolutionary forces who were very different from the pomp and discipline of his military forces. Many officers and infantrymen alike were denied continuance in the Piedmont army and a chance of pursuing their dream of liberating Rome and Venice. Many of the *Garibaldini* lost confidence in the monarchy and returned home to their civil occupations.

Garibaldi was utterly disgusted with the treatment of his men and decided to retire to Caprera. He took a sack of seed, some coffee and sugar, a bale of dried fish and a supply of macaroni—a meager reward for such a momentous and historical accomplishment. At dawn of 9 November, Garibaldi and his son, Menotti, departed Naples aboard the steamer *Washington*. Before he left, he paid a visit to English Admiral Mundy aboard the *Hannibal*. "I shall never be satisfied," he told the Admiral, "till emancipation from foreign rule has been effected throughout the entirety of the Italian kingdom. Rome and Venice are not French and Austrian cities. They are Italian cities. They belong to Italy alone." He dejectedly returned to Caprera as poor a man as when he had left in the spring, not sure his heroic tasks—bringing down a kingdom, abolishing an ancient dynasty, and altering the political configuration of the Italian peninsula—had been appreciated.

Kingdom of Piedmont/Italy, November 1860

CHAPTER XX: RETURN TO CAPRERA

The rigors of a barren, insular environment had not changed and Garibaldi welcomed the Spartan existence to forget his recent disappointments. He was now fifty-three years old and wracked with arthritic disabilities and pain. Despite this, after a few months of hard labor, Garibaldi's demeanor improved and the dark cloud of disillusionment slowly left. He was, in his own words, happy at Caprera in the solitude and immersed into the manual labor that the island demanded. It was back to nature and the elements—earth, sun, sea, sky, and the impregnable rock of his small domain that gave him faith in the normal occurrence of events.. A newborn calf was received as others would receive a child in the family. Great pride emanated from the simplest of tasks—wine made from his island grapes, a successful fruit-producing graft, beautiful blooms of planted bulbs, flowers and vegetables produced from homegrown seeds, etc. Caprera was becoming his paradise away from the trials and tribulations of the outside world.

Meanwhile, Giuseppe Garibaldi's name flashed all over the world in rightful recognition of his accomplishments. Admiration was mixed with downright astonishment that he could have ceded all he had won to his king. In the 1860s, there was no more popular figure in the western world; his achievements had spread across the world like wildfire. As a result, visitors and tourists stopped by the island regularly to shake hands or get a glimpse of this megahero. After a while, this was an imposition and Garibaldi became less friendly with uninvited strangers who upset his daily regimen. He did, however, receive influential dignitaries who desired to remain close to the general and his obvious power. Unbeknownst to him, Garibaldi had become an uncrowned king of Italy and was the nucleus of a new political force. He was regarded as if he were the head of new religion—a guru of libertarianism, so to speak.

On 18 April 1861, Garibaldi left his island hideaway to address the Piedmont parliament. When he stood to address the heavily attended assembly, he launched on a brutal tirade against Cavour for his abysmal treatment of his volunteers and accused him of fomenting unrest and possible civil war in southern Italy. Prime Minister Cavour responded with equal rage and insipid rancor; he demanded an immediate apology. Angry cries emanated from both sides of the aisle; the galleries were vociferous. The session was suspended in total disarray and disorder.

Upon reconvening, Garibaldi apologized to Cavour in hopes the prime minister would make use of his volunteers. Cavour said nothing. He refused to be compromised and dictated to by a man he regarded his inferior. Again, Garibaldi rebuked the reticent Cavour to the encouragement of his supporters, but without success. The general stood and, with a flippant gesture of swishing his poncho over his shoulder, stormed out of the hall. The "King of Caprera" returned to his island sanctuary reinforced, more than ever, in his distrust of politicians.

Some weeks later, ironically, Cavour suffered a stroke and died on 6 June. Consequently, Piedmont and Italy were without effective leadership for years. He had deservedly earned the reputation of being one of the most skillful European statesmen of the nineteenth century. It was at this time that Garibaldi corresponded with the United States and President Abraham Lincoln.

After the first battle of Bull Run, the Union Army had been reduced to a pitiful state. Lincoln desperately needed an infusion of men and military strategy to improve the Federal position. There was not a more qualified man in the world than Giuseppe Garibaldi. The general received feelers from the consul in Antwerp and Garibaldi encouraged the Americans with his favorable response, although he was adamant about the Union's position on slavery. The Emancipation Proclamation had not been signed into law as yet. On 7 September, the United States Minister in Belgium, Henry Sanford, traveled to Caprera and discussed the situation with Garibaldi. Subsequent to this meeting, a long and detailed report was forwarded to Lincoln. Garibaldi would join the fight to abolish slavery in America if certain prerequisites were met: He was to be appointed Commander-in-Chief of his forces, answering to no one other than Lincoln, and Lincoln must sign a proclamation against slavery. Garibaldi felt the two sides were fighting for material gain under the guise of a slavery issue. He did not want to get involved in a true civil war and, in his distrust of politicians, needed a written decree.

Soon after, the press got wind of this and headlines around the world were aglow with those correspondences. Reactions were varied from different corners of the world. The Italian government and King Victor Emmanuel gave their blessing; they were anxious to get rid of Garibaldi and his volunteers. Most papers in America were enthusiastic, but the *New York Times* wrote. "We trust that the war will not go on long enough to make his participation necessary."

In October 1862, after other entreaties by the American diplomatic corps, Garibaldi responded again to Lincoln and reiterated his preconditions; there was to be no movement upon his part until there was a clear proclamation freeing the slaves. It is pure speculation to say that Garibaldi induced Lincoln to act, but the Emancipation Proclamation was signed into law on 1 January 1863. But Lincoln's Chief of Staff refused to accept his other prerequisite—the independence of his forces under direct command of the president. In time, there was less and less chance of Garibaldi taking part in the American Civil War, although many of his followers did. In fact, a volunteer regiment was formed in New York—the Thirty-Ninth—and was called the "Garibaldi Guard." Garibaldi turned his attention to the Italian mainland and the renewed interest in liberating Rome and Venice.

Early in 1862, Garibaldi traveled to Turin and had consultations with King Victor Emmanuel and Prime Minister Urbano Ratazi. The complete context of these historic meetings is not known, but Garibaldi was given access to one million lire for an expedition to the Balkans against Austria. Enthralled by this recent encouragement, Garibaldi toured Lombardy and Piedmont soliciting men for this impending excursion. This tour was at the direction and expense of the government, and he was officially received by mayors and prefects. Passionate patriotic speeches preceded the most sophisticated banquets. Garibaldi enjoyed all this attention and believed the national pulse was beating for acquisition of Venice and Rome.

He arrived at Trescore and its healing waters for treatment of arthritis that had flared up in the cold temperatures of the north. A secret meeting convened of his most ardent supporters, lieutenants and chiefs of staff. Garibaldi presented the taking of Venice via Dalmatia and the Balkans but with governmental ties. The meeting was in turmoil from the start; the caucus was opposed to strings attached to the government and suspected a plot to get Garibaldi out of Italy. There was a strong feeling that the government had a pact with France to sacrifice him on some dangerous expedition. They preferred to wait for assurances that Venice was ready for a "Garibaldian" war of liberation.

Government spies reported to Ratazzi about the clandestine meeting. He was becoming increasingly anxious as to the direction of Garibaldi and his volunteers. Paris and Vienna were also concerned and pressured the Piedmont monarchy to curtail the actions of Garibaldi. Government forces surrounded Garibaldi's residence in Trescore; hostilities broke out between the volunteers and the Piedmont army. On 15 May, Colonel Nullo and a hundred volunteers were arrested at Sarnico and imprisoned, some of them were killed attempting to escape at Como.

Garibaldi was livid at the connivance of the government in this action against the *Garibaldini*. Speaking over the dead at Como, he charged Ratazzi with complicity and accused him of deliberately bringing him out of retirement on a dead-end excursion into the Balkans. He spoke passionately of his fallen comrades and, very moved, failed to continue the eulogy. The government used its influence to block a parliamentary inquiry into what really happened and, subsequently, they dropped prosecution and released all prisoners. However, the separation between Left and Right in Italy had widened.

Garibaldi quietly returned to Caprera.

CHAPTER XXI: DEFEAT AT ASPROMONTE

Suddenly, in June 1862, Garibaldi arrived in Palermo singularly determined to settle the "Roman question." A tumultuous frenzy greeted him upon his arrival, a swell of adoration built to a tidal wave of idolatry. The great "liberator" was heralded with the same ardor as their patron saint, Santa Rosalia. Garibaldi was encouraged by the reception and began a series of fiery speeches to rally the partisans to a campaign against Rome. "*Roma o morte!*" ("Rome or death!") was the Sicilian slogan, repeated in the streets of Palermo and the churches of Marsala, that spurred Garibaldi to higher levels of bellicose rhetoric. In a fervid tone, he reminded the people, "The plebiscites which had constituted Italy in 1860 had voted for a united kingdom— that is to say, they had been a conditional vote, and sovereignty would revert to the people if the government did not soon win Venice and Rome." This was considered a most seditious statement by the government.

However, the peasantry in Sicily would follow him anywhere and, in a short time, Garibaldi recruited three thousand volunteers. At his side were Corrao, Nullo, and Eber; noticeably absent were Bixio, Cosenz, Medici, and Türr who had succeeded in getting commissions into the regular Piedmont army. Medici wrote to him and warned, ". . . the road you are taking leads inevitably to civil war." Garibaldi would not heed his detractors and was determined to complete his mission. On 3 August, in reference to Garibaldi's movements, the government issued a proclamation, ". . . disowning the entire operation and that whosoever defied the royal directive would be liable to prosecution under the law." Garibaldi ignored all protestations and, on 20 August, marched east to Catania where he was accepted without a shot being fired. At this time, Garibaldi revealed a mysterious metal box that contained an important document with a red seal. He showed this to any official who questioned his movements, which made them assume the king's proclamation was a necessary protection against diplomatic protests. It was more certain to the government officers that Garibaldi did have some sort of approval from the king when the naval forces at Catania overlooked the preparations for invasion. Garibaldi crammed three thousand volunteers in two boats and crossed the Strait of Messina to Calabria without incident.

When the volunteers began to march north to Reggio, alarms sounded all over Europe. Turin and Prime Minister Ratazzi were at odds as what to do; they feared the intervention of other countries, especially France, the protector of the Vatican. Ratazzi tried to convince Louis-Napoleon that the only way to stop the progress of Garibaldi northward was to allow Italian troops to occupy Rome and protect the Pope. Napoleon III would not fall for such an obvious Cavourian ploy and pressured Victor Emmanuel to stop Garibaldi's northern progress. More than simply concerned about foreign interference, Piedmont was fearful of Garibaldi's popularity and his ability to rouse the people, which may lead to civil war. General Cialdini, stationed in Naples, was ordered to intercept Garibaldi and put an immediate end to his advancement. Cialdini cabled Colonel Pallavicini in Reggio and directed him to "leave with a column of six or seven battalions, to make every effort to overtake Garibaldi, and to attack and destroy him if he offers battle."

On 27 August, the rear guard of Garibaldi's forces was attacked above Reggio and they scurried to the mountain range of Aspromonte. The next morning only five hundred men were at Garibaldi's command, as many had deserted or lost their way. However, they were in a strong defensive position and could have fended off their attackers, but Garibaldi would have none of it. A battle at this juncture would pit Italians against Italians and lead to civil war. In a daze at this probability, he was astonished when the government forces attacked and his men returned fire. Garibaldi was overcome with grief for his mother country and her brave sons. Fearlessly, he walked out in the open center of the skirmish and shouted, "*Non fate fuoco! Non fate fuoco!*" ("*Don't Fire! Don't Fire!*"); like a crazed man, he kept pleading until the bugler blew the "Cease Fire." Suddenly, he grabbed his thigh and crumpled to the ground; he had been shot in the left thigh and in the right foot. He was carried to the shade of a chestnut tree and gingerly laid down next to his son, Menotti, who also had been wounded. Garibaldi's wounds did not seem to be life threatening, but they were extremely painful. He was approached by an arrogant lieutenant of the enemy on horseback who demanded that the general surrender. Garibaldi chastised the officer for his lack of military protocol. Colonel Pallavicini soon arrived and, with hat in hand and in the most humble way, asked for Garibaldi's unconditional surrender. It must have presented a pitiful picture—this magnanimous Italian reduced to an old, wounded, defenseless soldier at the mercy of the government that owed its power to the very people that Garibaldi freed.

Mounted on a stretcher, he was carried down the mountainside to Scilla, with the bullet still lodged in his foot, and imprisoned on a charge of treason. In Turin, anxious legislators were hesitant to bring him to trial, mainly because it would reveal the complicity of the king and, more importantly, because of the immense popularity of Garibaldi. Sympathy and support poured in from all over the world, and the king was pressured to grant amnesty to Garibaldi. Although some of his collaborators were executed, he was granted a pardon on 11 October.

However, he could not travel and his supporters were concerned for his health, as the bullet in his foot had not been removed. An excess of twenty of Europe's finest surgeons were consulted, but none could extricate the bullet. The attempts only worsened Garibaldi's physical condition, as it was what modern surgery would call overt butchery. Amputation was considered to save his life. Finally, on 23 November, a Tuscan surgeon, Professor Zanetti, removed the metal ball to the delight of his supporters and especially Garibaldi, who underwent the operation without anesthesia, a full eighty-seven days after he had been shot. On the afternoon of 20 December 1862, he sailed home to Caprera.

CHAPTER XXII: ENGLAND/VENICE

Garibaldi returned to the cold, barren island of Caprera to recuperate from his wounds, physical and emotional. He was bedridden for months, unable to tend to his farm. In addition, his arthritis became even more severe and increased his disability. It was not until the fall of 1863 that he could get around the island carried in a bath chair, ultimately hobbling about on crutches. It took years to heal the wound on his foot, as fragments of bone continually exited and kept the lesion open. Physically and morally, he was a beaten man; it was not easy to dismiss the defeat at Aspromonte.

During this time, friends and visitors from all over the world paid homage to the megahero at his island hideaway. Some he failed to see, claiming illness, but others, favored because of their politics or sex, he welcomed readily. One of these, Mrs. Chambers, a representative of an English committee, urged him to come to England. At first, he was not in favor of such a trip, but after much deliberation thought it could be beneficial for many reasons. He was seeking support for the liberation of Rome and Venice. He had grandiose plans for the liberation of Poland and Greece, and he even aspired to intervene in favor of Denmark against Austria. Subsequently, with Mrs. Chambers, the general's physician, Basle, and his sons, Menotti and Ricciotti, Garibaldi boarded the steamer *Ripon* and headed for England.

The *Ripon* docked at Southampton on a rainy Sunday, 3 April 1864, and was greeted by a tumultuous crowd of thousands. Ships in the harbor were bedecked with British and Italian flags; horns and whistles were blown with excitement. The pier was crowded with well-wishers and admirers shouting, "*Viva*

Garibaldi! Viva Garibaldi!" Garibaldi simply doffed his cap. Duke Sutherland and officials of the welcoming committee whisked him away to the mayor's home, where the Prince of Wales, Gladstone (the Chancellor of the Exchequer), Tennyson, Florence Nightingale, and the students of Eton visited him.

Garibaldi arrived in London on 11 April to an even larger reception. In fact, no other figure in prior history had ever received a more majestic welcome. Over a half million people lined the streets of his procession; throngs of admirers were positioned on rooftops, on balconies, at windows. They waited for hours to get a glimpse of their hero. It took the cortege six hours to reach the Stafford House, as Garibaldi's carriage was smothered with adulators anxious to shake his hand or kiss his coat. He remained virtually a prisoner in the Stafford House, receiving notables from all over the world by way of banquets, ceremonies, and balls. Notably absent was an invitation from Queen Victoria, who resented his notoriety. As the hysteria over his presence increased, visits from high ranking officials decreased.

Garibaldi was not comfortable in this environment, such eminence kept him from mingling with the common people. He did have time to meet with Mazzini, as well as other noted European agitators, which disturbed the continent's leaders. However, no one in legitimate and diplomatic circles gave him much support in his other political interests. Suddenly, on 22 April, Garibaldi left England, with a stopover at Cornwall to visit Colonel Peard, and returned to Caprera. Although the British people took him to their hearts, he was disappointed that his sojourn to England proved fruitless. There were smoldering intrigues that required his attention at home and he had Italian allies to support them.

Soon after he returned in May 1864, he summoned his lieutenants and commanders to the island of Ischia under the pretense of treatment (mud baths) for his arthritic condition. Despite the negative treatment of Garibaldi and his men following the defeat at Aspromonte, it seems that he had been approached by messengers of the king to open a new front at the rear of the Austrian forces in Galica. His chiefs were strongly opposed to such a futile undertaking. The aims of Victor Emmanuel were still under suspicion. While it was true Garibaldi was an enormous success with the populace in England, the Italian people revered him as somewhat of a demigod, which diminished the crown's ability to rule. The obvious, tactful move to tarnish this hero's image was to send him into a winless battle. Garibaldi and his staff were not to be taken in by the Machiavellian machinations of Victor Emmanuel II this time.

Caprera was to be a permanent residence for the general for the next two years. Farming on the island proved unprofitable and his health prevented him from increasing his yield or enjoying the fruits of his labor. The livestock were allowed to run wild and ate or damaged whatever crops did grow. A yacht that was given to him by a benefactor was allowed to deteriorate at its mooring by the elements. Mentally, Garibaldi was healthy and strong, but bored and restless; he desired the excitement of battle. He considered going to Mexico to join Benito Juarez in his quest for independence against Emperor Maximilian. He requested permission from the king to govern the newly acquired south—Naples, Calabria, Sicily, etc. The governing body of the king and the Italian parliament had made a travesty of human rights in Sicilian and Neapolitan transactions and they were close to civil war. The request was denied emphatically. Still, Garibaldi's mind was occupied with thoughts of national concern—Rome, Venice, and Italian unity.

Finally in 1866, a solution to the Venice question brought Garibaldi back into Italian affairs. The Italian government had entered into an alliance with Prussia, who had designs on Austria. Austria offered to cede Venice in the condition that Italy would not enter the hostilities aligned with the German warlord, Otto von Bismarck. However, Italy wanted to exert its position as a nation and also acquire the lands of Italian speaking Trieste and Tyrol, as well as Venice. Rome would have to be put on the back-burner for now, as Napoleon III kept constant vigil over the Papal States. Arms and munitions were ordered into production; taxes were levied to support this effort.

At first, no government officials contacted Garibaldi, as they did not want him back on the scene again. They feared his immense popularity with the populace. Against the advice of General La Marmora, the new prime minister, the king sent word to Garibaldi that authorized his leadership of a command that would attack the rear of the Austrian forces at Dalmatia; it was a resurfacing of the planned expedition of 1864. Garibaldi was pleased with the idea of a separate command in a remote area, away from the interfering Piedmont generals who were jealous of his military successes. Nevertheless, the prime minister changed the general's area of engagement to Tyrol, successively keeping him farther away from the main military action at Venice.

Garibaldi left his island sanctuary on 10 June to establish his headquarters at Salo on Lake Garda, but huge difficulties were experienced in resurrecting his band of freedom fighters. The *Garibaldini* could have recruited more than 100,000 men, but the governmental recruiting centers sent thousands of volunteers home. The government did not want Garibaldi to have such a large force at his disposal following the cessation of hostilities; they limited his force to thirty-five thousand men. They were allowed to wear the red shirts of the *Garibaldini*, but the government sent the poorest equipment—old rifles, disused cannons, faulty munitions, etc. Although the bulk of his former staff was still with the Regular Army, Garibaldi managed to assemble an impressive General Staff consisting of Fabrizio, Bertani, Missori, his son, Menotti, and his son-in-law, Canzio.

Generals La Marmora and Cialdini of the governmental forces were in charge of the main campaign against Venice. Due to horrendous military judgment, they met a disastrous defeat at Custoza at the hands of the Austrians; the Italian forces were in disarray. To make matters worse, the navy was humiliated near the island of Lissa on 20 July. It seemed the Italian establishment had failed in its first attempt to join the League of Nations. It was unable to exert its will, either militarily or diplomatically, over another.

However, Garibaldi was recording successes, one by one,

in the north. The *Garibaldini* pressed the enemy relentlessly. They won at Monte Suello, at Caffaro, at Forte Ampolla, and at Bezzecca. At Bezzecca, the *Garibaldini* lost 2,382 men and Garibaldi was wounded early in the campaign. Garibaldi's victories were the only succor to the Italian spirit after the defeat of the Regular Army at Custoza because of inept military stratagem. The road to Trent and the belly of Austria lay open to his forces when Garibaldi received a wire from General La Marmora with orders to withdraw from the hinterland of Tyrol. Peace had come.

Garibaldi obeyed but was furious with the order. His men were overwhelmed with rancor toward the military judgment that sent so many of their brethren to their deaths, only to stop when complete victory was within their grasp. Peace had come at a price. Austria had made peace with Prussia on 23 August and Italy on 3 October. However, Austria ceded Venice to France and regained Trieste and Trent. Napoleon III, in turn, signed Venice over to Victor Emmanuel in a pact that repudiated Italy's claim to Rome. Florence was to be the new capital of Italy. With these assurances, France removed its defending forces from the Papal States. Italy could have acquired Venice without a shot before the war. The Italian government must be branded with negligence for such a parody of military intelligence.

Garibaldi continued to tour Italy with fervent speeches against Rome, condemning all priests, ". . . the scourge of Italy," and against the Papacy, ". . . the negation of God." He roused the enthusiasm of the populace and proved to himself that his call for national action could be heard. He even believed the government approved of his stirring the masses to take action against Rome.

However, the government could not allow Garibaldi to create such a furor for the acquiescence of Rome. Under the pact with France (The Convention of September), Italy had now to recognize the Pope's sovereignty. Early in 1867, under pressure from Napoleon III, the Italian government arrested Garibaldi and returned him to Caprera.

CHAPTER XXIII: DEFEAT AT MENTENA

Giuseppe Garibaldi turned sixty years old on 4 July 1867. Despite his obvious aging—his hair had thinned and become white, his face had a pallor that mirrored his pain from arthritis— his spirit was fervent with the desire to acquire Rome, the final piece to the Italian Republic pie. He avowed his sons, Menotti and Ricciotti, to continue his efforts on the mainland. The government, by their constant duplicity, encouraged Garibaldi to pursue his dream. However, they wanted him to remain, for a time, inactive to prove to Europe that Italy was honoring the "Convention of September 1866."

A plan was formulated to initiate some sort of insurrection in the Roman province and give the government an excuse to enter to bring peace. In October, several bands of *Garibaldini* crossed into Papal territory and staged a revolt. Unfortunately, the Romans remained impassive to the whole escapade and did not lift a finger to aid the revolutionaries. Garibaldi, at home at Caprera, was appalled at this indifference and deemed a spark of revolt needed his presence to spread the fire of rebellion.

Security at Caprera was intensive; a blockade of up to eight ships watched Garibaldi's every move. A scheme was devised for him to escape from exile and join his coconspirators in Rome. A close friend, similar in size and dressed in Garibaldi's farming clothes, walked the island in crutches. Meanwhile, Garibaldi stained his beard black and rowed to a neighboring island under the protection of darkness. At Maddalena, he rode horseback the length of the island and secured a longboat to reach the northern shore of Sardinia. He eventually rendezvoused with his son-in-law, Canzio, and boarded a steamer for Italy. Garibaldi arrived in Florence on 20 October to the insincere surprise of the government. It was the scheme of Premier Ratazzi to use Garibaldi and his popularity to plant the seed of revolution in the hearts of the Roman populace. He would drive home the point to Europe that the Roman forces could not secure the frontier of the Papa States. He tried to impress Louis-Napoleon that Rome would benefit from the security of the Piedmont forces and the Italian Republic. However, Louis-Napoleon was not taken in by this subterfuge and ordered the French army back into Italy to defend the Pope. Subsequently, Victor Emmanuel feared that the actions of the *Garibaldini* would result in a full scale war with France and ordered the arrest of Garibaldi. Premier Ratazzi resigned in disapproval. Garibaldi was abandoned once again.

Before the arrest could be carried out, the general prepared for invasion of the Papacy. He stubbornly refused to be dissuaded. Friends and officers were adamant with their of disapproval of such an huge undertaking. France was sending countless troops to defend Rome. Determined, with or without government or friends' approval, he and the *Garibaldini* marched south. However, a new prime minister, General Menabrèa, ordered the immediate apprehension of Garibaldi and deployed government forces to that end.

The *Garibaldini* had initial success at Monterotondo, but the local populace did not come to assist the revolutionary forces, which was incomprehensible to Garibaldi. An historian wrote, "The passivity with which Rome awaited its destiny was a great enigma and source of worry for Garibaldi. He had based his strategy, as usual, on the assumption that he would have abundant popular support; without it he could do nothing. He knew from experience that a voluntary militia will grow rapidly when it has the good will and the enthusiasm of the masses on its side, but will shrink just as rapidly when it has to contend with the apathy or, worse, the hostility of civilians." Other incursions into Rome, most notably by the Cairoli brothers, met heroic deaths at the walls of Rome. Garibaldi moved into the outskirts of Rome, but was beaten back to Monterotondo. The French were amassing in greater numbers and had superior rifles, cannons, and ammunition.

It was Sunday morning at Porta Pia of Rome when a Franco-Pontifical combined force of seven thousand marched out to engage the Red-shirts. Garibaldi left Monterotondo for the neighboring town of Mentena and joined the main body of his forces by three o'clock in the afternoon. They met resistance almost immediately. The French pounced upon them with their new rapid repeating rifles, Chassepots, and smothered the *Garibaldini* with intense fire. Garibaldi's ammunition dwindled to an embarrassing minimum. The call to retreat was sounded. The defeat at Mentena on 3 November brought to a close the Roman Campaign of 1867. The *Garibaldini* lost six hundred killed and 1,700 captured.

Recriminations were widespread. The king, the government, and even the Mazzinians were blamed. The lack of support from the Roman populace was singularly the most important factor for the failure of this expedition. The new French Chassepot rifle, the lack of arms and equipment of the *Garibaldini*, the undisciplined volunteers, and the false euphoria of the enlisted men—who thought all they had to do to take Rome was to enter it but deserted after the first casualty—were responsible for the defeat as well. The Red-shirts' staff of experienced commanders was even chastised, but, most of all, Garibaldi blamed himself. Due to his age and crippling arthritic condition, he was unable to lead his men into battle. He no longer represented the dashing, heroic figure upon a white charger rallying his forces under insurmountable odds as he had done in the past. No longer were the *Garibaldini* led by the charismatic, flamboyant, death-defying warrior that Garibaldi once was.

Garibaldi and his most loyal supporters managed to slip across the Papal border. He ordered a special train for the remnants of his command and departed for the western shore of Italy. Unfortunately, the train was stopped at Figline by government forces and Garibaldi was forcibly removed from his seat amid strong protestations of other passengers. Garibaldi admonished the arresting officer, Lt. Colonel Camozzi, by saying, "You are aware that you are committing an illegality. I am guilty of no act against the Italian State or against its laws. Nor have you caught me committing any crime. You have no right to arrest me, and I refuse to yield to an act of violence." Nevertheless, after a few minutes of hesitation, he was whisked off to the fortress at Varignano with members of his family—Menotti, Ricciotti, and Canzio. An amnesty was granted almost immediately; news of Garibaldi's arrest would certainly incite protests and disorder. The Italian parliament could not take a chance of a trial which, in all probability, would show the government's complicity. After he agreed to leave Italy and abstain from further insurrection, Garibaldi was returned to Caprera.

Disillusionment had to be the mood of Garibaldi at this time. Many times, he was encouraged by the government to go into action and every time he was thwarted by the government's duplicity. He realized that politics in the nineteenth century were amoral and that any means, however unscrupulous, can justifiably be used in achieving political power was the credo of the Italian government. He strongly felt he was placed in jeopardy by the government in the expedition of 1867 to have him killed or humiliated, ultimately to get rid of him. He was ashamed that the new Italian nation for which so many young, brave Italians had given their lives was being abused by a gang of self-serving politicians.

CHAPTER XXIV: FRENCH EXPEDITION

Garibaldi remained a prisoner on his island for the next three years, bitter in his resentment toward all who had failed him. He was becoming increasingly vociferous in his condemnation of the Italian government, the Pope, Mazzini, Victor Emmanuel, and all politicians. Ambassadors and foreign correspondents that visited Caprera were subjected to his endless tirades. This all came from the disillusionment created from years of duplicity and the unfulfilled expectation of a united Italy in his lifetime; his age and disability did not help, either. His arthritic condition was becoming much worse. He often used crutches to hobble around the island, but his hands had become so gnarled that he could not write or sign his name. Occasionally, his ankle wound would reopen and fester.

However, this cynicism and black mood were not directed to his family and friends. He was still a simple man, amiable and good-natured at home. He kept busy trying to cultivate his small farm, tending to his endeared livestock and rearing his newborn children. Through a secretary, he wrote compassionate letters to past comrades and their families. Other vituperative correspondence was directed to the aforementioned "enemies of Italy."

This was the period that his anticlerical feelings intensified; he blamed the Papacy for the continued disunification of Italy. He derided Catholicism and its priests for clinging to the temporal power of the Pope and the effeminacy of the Italian male. He was not an atheist. Rather, he was a religious man believing in a loving God and not in the "vengeful, angry, unjust, and cruel God of the priests." The Catholic Church, on the other hand, refused any compromise and distanced itself from the trend of liberalism. They refused Britain's offer to relocate to Malta or some other remote site.

In his idleness, Garibaldi began to write his first novel, *Clelia*, with the aid of a secretary. It was a poor attempt, but he was encouraged by his friends to have it published. The manuscript reflected the honesty and sincerity of the author and did not make for exciting reading. It was a simple tale of "eight noble-minded lovers" who met their deaths at Mentena. He wrote two other novels that barely need to be mentioned. Garibaldi's writing aptitude was more suited to proclamations and editorials where he could vent his spleen at those who transgressed against him and Italy. *Memoirs* was his best book and allowed him to relive the fire and determination of his younger years— oratorical, declamatory, and intense was his tone. He even tried his hand at poetry in French and Italian; it was amateurish but he was encouraged by the false flattery of friends.

In 1870, Louis-Napoleon of France found himself in a desperate fight to preserve the French Republic. As a result of a of series of provocative exchanges with Prussia concerning the rightful heir to the Spanish throne, war broke out between the two powerful nations. Unfortunately, France was not prepared for these hostilities and received staggering defeats at the hands of the warlike Prussians. The Emperor himself was captured at Sedan along with 170,000 men on 2 September 1870. The French forces in Rome were recalled to protect Paris and Metz. An Italian newspaper wrote, "Within a few days the French will be gone from the patrimony of St. Peter. The Pope will be left to face his subjects. This is a most advantageous situation, one which will probably lead to the definitive solution of the Roman Question, if only our government finds a way to act with the necessary prudence and boldness."

The Italian government did grasp the initiative and invaded the Papal States on 11 September. Garibaldi was told to keep away from Rome and his every move was closely watched. After little Pontifical resistance, troops under the leadership of former *Garibaldini*, Bixio and Cosenz, entered Rome on 20 September. Rome would become the capital of Italy. The unification of

Italy was now complete.

The old general at Caprera was not excited by these sudden turn of events. He was disappointed that he was not asked to join the taking of Rome, but, more importantly, he deemed it deplorable that it was done over someone's misfortune. In fact, his compassion turned to France, who was in danger of a catastrophic defeat. He always defended the French revolution and its subsequent democratic state—it was Napoleon III that he loathed. He directed a letter to the French Republic and offered his services in their time of need, but no reply was received. Not to be denied, he sailed for Marseilles aboard the *Ville de Paris* and was joined by a few thousand Italians. It was not received as a great call to arms by most Italians; many still hated the French for their political machinations that blunted the Roman acquisition of 1867. He landed in Marseilles on 7 October to a hero's welcome. He replied to the crowd, "This the second time I have come to Marseilles. The first time, I had been condemned to death by my country's oppressors and you generously gave me asylum. Now I have come to repay my debt to France, to cooperate in freeing her territory from the Prussian hordes and in raising once again the glorious banner of the Republic."

The French had no choice but to give Garibaldi the command of about five thousand men. He made his sons, Menotti, and Ricciotti, brigade commanders in what was considered a ragged force, replete with undisciplined volunteers. A cold shoulder was received from the pompous French generals who regarded Garibaldi as an amateur and a foreigner, which made it difficult to satisfy the logistics of a successful military campaign.

At first, Garibaldi and the *Garibaldini* (still called *Garibaldini* though made up of mostly Frenchmen and other Europeans) did not embarrass themselves in an initial skirmish with a top Prussian general. In fact, compared to their French counterparts who were losing battle after battle, they seemed the most successful; they were responsible for the only French victories of the Franco-Prussian War. Garibaldi's leadership relied on his old offensive strategy of speed, deception, mobility, and quick decisions to make his force effective. Due to his successes, the French empowered him with a force of forty-thousand.

Garibaldi's forces were engaged in a great battle at Auton and Dijon and gaining momentum when word came through that the Germans had forced an armistice on 30 January 1871. Astonishingly, there was no provision in the armistice for the *Garibaldini* and the ground they held. The Germans wanted to settle a score with the *Garibaldini* who had bested them on several occasions. The French could not have cared less and abandoned them to their fate. Garibaldi and his men were left to fend for themselves. It did not require much military intelligence to realize Garibaldi and his men were in a precarious situation. They could not defend themselves against the entire might of the Prussian forces, who wanted to punish this foreigner and his mercenary army. The French washed their hands of the whole affair, so relieved that they had gained an armistice and offered no assistance. The *Garibaldini* began a speedy march at 7:00 o'clock in the morning of 31 January to Chagny to escape the closing net of the Prussians. Garibaldi, age sixty-three, wracked with arthritic pain and unable to mount a horse, walked his men eventually to Bourg and to freedom. He did not lose one man in his retreat and on 1 March the volunteers were demobilized.

Surprisingly, Garibaldi was elected in six provinces to the French National Assembly in Bordeaux, the provisional seat of the new government. Despite his aversion to politics, he went to the convention in hopes of striking a chord for republicanism and to plead the case of his comrades who had been wounded and abandoned by France. When he walked into the great hall of the Grand Theater at 2:00 P.M. on 13 February, jeers greeted him. To the elected officials and not to the electorate, he was a foreigner, an anti-papist, and tagged as a socialist. The president read Garibaldi's letter of resignation. ". . . As my last duty to the Republic I have come to Bordeaux, where the representatives of the nation have convened. But I must renounce the honor to which I have been elected."

Following the reading, the general, in his Pampas attire and plumed hat, rose to speak. Someone from the rear of the hall shouted, "Take off your hat!" With that, all hell broke out on the floor of the convention hall; the Left, in defense of Garibaldi, confronted the Right. The assembly transformed into an unruly mob and prevented Garibaldi from continuing his speech. He turned for the door and left in disgust. He was humiliated by such a poor display of democratic action and immediately returned to Caprera by way of Marseilles. Later, Victor Hugo, the celebrated novelist, addressed the parliament and spoke in defense of his friend. "Three weeks ago you refused to listen to Garibaldi. Today you refuse to listen to me. I shall go and speak far away from here." Hugo imposed a self-exile on himself and never returned to France again, the land of his birth.

France must bear the blame for such deplorable treatment of a heroic figure who extended his hand in their hour of need. The National Defense Government of France deserted him when it could be proven that their position at the end of the war would have been more desperate without the services of Garibaldi. It's obvious that his intervention was not appreciated. He had simply followed his most inner values for freedom and independence. Since the first military episodes in the Rio Grande, his first priority was freedom for individuals and nations. This concern was not restricted to Italy alone but to peoples everywhere. Internationalism and peace among democratic nations were his utopia.

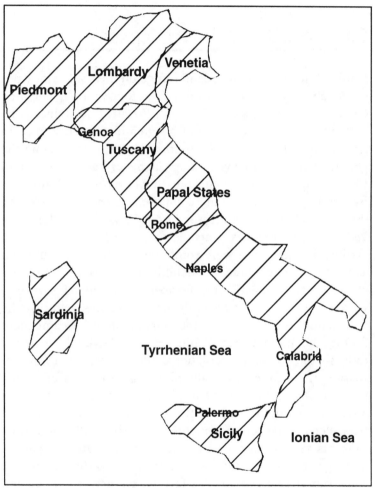

Kingdom of Italy, November 1870

CHAPTER XXV: FINAL YEARS

Garibaldi returned to his island refuge on the cold, windy day of 16 February 1871, the birthday of his four-year-old daughter, Clelia. He had fathered Clelia in 1867 after he seduced the eighteen-year-old wet-nurse of his granddaughter. Francesca Armosino was a plain peasant girl from Asti who became the general's island lover, even though he never was divorced from the unconsummated marriage to Marchesina Raimondi. Francesca bore him two more children—Rosita, in 1869 (she died in 1871 before he returned from France) and Manlio, in 1873. He was sixty-six years old when he had his last child. Garibaldi's later years were comforted by these new children as well as twenty-three grandchildren. His daughter Teresa, alone, had fourteen offspring. Garibaldi returned to his writings with renewed vigor. Aware of the debility of advancing age, he was anxious to complete his memoirs before he became more feeble and memory failed him. He was involved in many causes—the Socialist International, the International Court of Justice, trade unions, female education, abolition of capital punishment, and a scheme to divert the course of the Tiber after draining the swamps of the Campagna. Although he had been elected to seven parliaments in Italy since 1860, he seldom took his seat, preferring to send a subordinate to read his message. These directives were patronizing in their content to some but arrogant toward his favorite targets—the Pope and politicians. He remained consistent in his beliefs, though he was cut off from the mainstream and alone on the island with his thoughts.

Garibaldi remained a romantic socialist, idealistic in his belief that the populace must be loved before anyone can successfully rule them, firm in his assumption that the current movement of national ambitions would lead to a federal union, resolute in his advocacy of a dictatorship for a time to offset the corruption of self-serving politicians and ineffective parliaments. This was recognized as typical Garibaldi dogma, but revered by his followers. However, he was taken seriously concerning his stand on Italy's neglect of the South, the initiation of social and educational reform, the problems of brigandage and its cures, the dilemma of the starving poor, and the huge sums spent on colonization rather than on the needs of Italy. He was for the constant struggle of man, people and countries fighting against ruling class inequities and the eventual polarization of values; against the subordination of the people's will by politicians greed and their covert pacts subjugating the people's wants and desires. He was adamant in his belief that life is not for the privileged, but for the ordinary man. The ennobled, the gifted, and the intelligent should have an unrestrained voice in the government of the populace. This, and only this, would secure the sanctity of a popular forum.

In private life, he remained a simple, gentle, courteous, loving man untouched by his celebrity; he was the most heralded hero of the time. The stoic picture of himself dressed in his S. A. poncho and red blouse adorned a myriad of homes throughout the world next to icons and pictures of the Messiah. This constant adoration had to affect him somewhat; he believed in his "press clippings" and enjoyed reading about himself. He was always a serious man and never took anything lightly; his character was devoid of a sense of humor.

Many benefactors tried to lavish gifts upon Garibaldi, but he stubbornly resisted their advances. But, here in his old age, he was close to poverty and heavily in debt after guaranteeing a business loan for Menotti. The new Italian government offered a sizable remuneration for his dedicated years of service, which the venerable general was forced to accept, after much protestation. "I never thought I should be reduced to the state of a pensioner," he said sadly. As soon as the money arrived, he dispersed all of it. He paid off Menotti's bank loan, absolved other debts, bequeathed various amounts on Francesca and the children, and lent the remainder to his friend, Luigio Orlando, who faced bankruptcy. Other events occurred to depress him in his waning years. In 1875, he received a pitiful letter from his daughter Anita, the illegitimate offspring with Battistina Ravello. Sixteen years old and living in Crete for her education with his friend Mme. Schwartz, she was maladjusted and desperately unhappy. She begged her father to allow her to return home. Menotti was ushered off to Crete to retrieve her. Anita arrived bedraggled and infested with body lice. Garibaldi was incensed at the condition of his daughter and wrote a strong reprimand to Mme. Schwartz, which she chose not to include in her memoirs. Unfortunately, Anita did not enjoy the reunion with her father and siblings for long. She was stricken with a high fever and bedridden. Physicians were hurriedly called in and the dreaded diagnosis of meningitis set a veil of gloom over Caprera. Anita did not recover and, two months after her return, she died.

Francesca Armosino, a peasant woman with country values, was insanely jealous of the constant procession of relatives, friends, and admirers that visited the general at Caprera. She was cool and even rude to these visitors while, at the same time, she doted on every wish and desire of Garibaldi. Consequently, fewer and fewer visitors came to the island, and some of Garibaldi's children opted to relocate to the mainland. Garibaldi did nothing to alter the flow of things and relegated himself to accept the status quo. In fact, he pursued the hope of marriage to Francesca to legitimatize his children by her. This was to be no easy task, as his marriage to the Marchesina Raimondi in 1860 was never dissolved.

He traveled to Rome in 1879 to secure an annulment of that marriage, but received little support. Victor Emmanuel had died in 1878 and the accession of King Humbert, his son, had changed the political climate. Prime Minister Benedetto Cairoli, the last of the five Cairoli brothers and a member of the Thousand, was unable to pass a decree in parliament to nullify the marital union. Francesco Crispi, an old friend and a political influence, represented Garibaldi in his petition and failed in his first attempt. Finally, on 14 January 1880, under great popular pressure, a favorable second decision was made by the high court of appeals and a formal decree of divorce was granted ". . . on the grounds that the contract had been made under Austrian law which permitted divorce in cases of nonconsummation."

The wedding on 14 January 1880 was a joyous day at Caprera. All of the general's family (except Ricciotti) as well as Francesca's relatives were present. Surrounded by his family and legitimizing the names of his children, Clelia and Manlio, Garibaldi was the happiest he had been in years. The past disappointments somehow seemed unimportant now in this moment of familial bliss. In a melancholic mood, he mused, "Mine has been a tempestuous life, made up—like most people's, I believe—of both good and evil. I may say that I have always sought the good, for myself and for my fellow men. If on any occasion I have done evil, I have done so involuntarily."

Garibaldi's health continued to deteriorate during those final years. His extremities were twisted from arthritis and he was moved about only in a wheelchair. His shock of long white hair and a pale, ashen complexion presented the image of a weak, old man. Doctors implored him to go to a better climate for his health. Only after increasing disability and pain did he agree to go to Naples for a time. Crowds surrounded his villa at Posillipo, hopeful to get a glimpse of their hero. Even though he was getting weaker, he insisted on visiting Sicily for the sexcentennial of the *Sicilian Vespers* in May 1882. The crowds were huge in Palermo as the silent, rather pathetic figure was carried through the streets upon a makeshift stretcher. The populace was in a hush and aghast at the condition of their "liberator." Mortality was never an option for their hero.

Shortly afterward, Garibaldi returned to Caprera close to death. On 1 June, a doctor was summoned from a nearby ship; the general was having difficulty breathing due to severe congestion. Giuseppe Garibaldi died on the afternoon of 2 June 1882, one month shy of his seventy-fifth birthday.

Epilogue

Garibaldi left instructions to be cremated in an open fire. He wanted to be burned like the great warriors of the past and added, "Only the priests oppose it. It hurts their trade." Francesca tried in all earnest to carry out the wishes of her husband, but to no avail. There was an enormous protest to prevent this ritual from being carried out on the great champion of Italian liberty. Government officials, friends, and the loyal populace, who revered the man in life, turned Francesca's head and a customary burial was planned. Giuseppe Garibaldi was buried near his house on Caprera, among a throng of relatives, friends, representatives of the royal family, government officials, military bureaucrats, and members of the international diplomatic corps. His coffin was carried to its final resting place by survivors of the Thousand.

Francesca stayed on at Caprera until her death in 1923. Menotti (1840-1903) and Ricciotti (1847-1923) became generals in the Italian army and led the *Garibaldini* in many military expeditions during their lifetime. Ricciotti sons led a Garibaldi Legion in World War I. Teresa and her husband, Stefano Canzio, left Caprera with their brood and spent their remaining years in Genoa. Clelia, who never married, remained in her father's house until her death in 1959, two months before her ninety-second birthday. Manlio, a lieutenant in the Italian navy, died at the young age of twenty-seven in 1900.

Caprera was designated as a national park in 1980 and is linked to the Isle of Maddalena by a causeway. Garibaldi's rustic home of twenty-six years is a popular museum with much of the original furniture and relics of the period. A steady procession of tourists and history aficionados visit Garibaldi's grave every year.

Many of the people who shared the limelight during those historic times with Garibaldi did not out live the general. Mazzini died in 1872; Napoleon III, after exile in England, died in 1873; Victor Emmanuel and the Pope (Pio Nono) in 1878. However, Mme. Schwartz lived until 1899 and was responsible for translating Garibaldi's *Memoirs* into German under the pen name of Elpis Melena.

The final details to the "Roman Question" were not settled until 1929. Mussolini and Pope Pius XI were instrumental in signing the Lateran Agreement. The Holy See (Vatican State) was designated as a separate entity within Rome, Italy and answerable to the state but had full liberty in all spiritual manners.

A referendum in June 1946 voted for an Italian Republic which doomed the fate of the monarchy. As a consequence, the arms of the House of Savoy that emblazoned the center of the Italian flag were removed. King Umberto, great-grandson of Victor Emmanuel, abdicated on 13 June, fled to Sardinian exile, and was never allowed to return to the mainland, even after his death. A constitution was finally ratified in December 1947 and the democratic Republic of Italy was born. Since that time, there have been in excess of fifty changes to the administrations and governments in Italy.

For the history buff, there is the Garibaldi-Meucci Museum in Staten Island maintained by the Order Sons of Italy in America. Meucci was the unrecognized inventor Garibaldi lived with during his four years in America (1850-1854). The museum is housed in the simple cottage where Meucci resided until his death in 1889 and is full of photographs, letters, clippings, and period lithographs of both men. A collection of Garibaldi's medals, weaponry, and one of his infamous red shirts can be found on display.

For the students of history, extended information on Giuseppe Garibaldi and the Italian Republic can be found in the bibliography listings at the end of this manuscript.

BIBLIOGRAPHY

de Polnay, Peter: *Garibaldi, the Legend and the Man*. London: Hollis and Carter, 1960.

Hearder, H. and D. P. Waley. *A Short History of Italy*. London: Cambridge University Press, 1963.

Hibbert, Christopher: *Garibaldi and His Enemies*. New York: Penguin Books Ltd., 1965.

Melena, Elpis. *Garibaldi's Memoirs*. Sarasota, Florida: International Institute of Garibaldian Studies, 1981.

Smith, Denis. *Garibaldi*. New York: Alfred Knopf, 1956.

Trevelyan, George. *Garibaldi and the Thousand*. New York: Longmans, Green & Co., 1909.

Trevelyan, George: *Garibaldi and the Making of Italy*. New York: Longmans, Green & Co., 1911.

Viotti, Andrea. *Garibaldi, the Revolutionary and His Men*. United Kingdom: Blandford Press Ltd., 1979.